ENDORSEMENTS

If you're interested in achieving financial and personal success, Money Remixed offers a wonderful blend of real-world advice, deep inspiration, and powerful insight. The authors take complex concepts and makes them simple and actionable.

—Marci Shimoff, #1 NY Times bestselling author, Happy for No Reason and Chicken Soup for the Woman's Soul

Money Remixed is a refreshing and comprehensive guide to cultivating a wealthy mindset and achieving true financial empowerment. The authors skillfully blend practical steps with insightful wisdom, offering readers a clear roadmap through the 14 steps to a wealthy mindset. From vision and purpose to managing fear and developing knowledge, this book is an invaluable resource for anyone ready to transform their financial reality and embrace a life of abundance. Highly recommended!

— Peggy McColl, New York Times Best-Selling Author

Money Remixed is an essential reading as it isn't just a book about wealth—it's a guide to living with purpose and financial clarity. The insights here are refreshingly practical and profound, offering a roadmap to help you align your financial goals with a greater sense of fulfillment. Every chapter provides not only actionable advice but a shift in perspective that truly empowers and transformative. This book is for anyone looking to redefine their relationship with money and unlock a mindset for lasting success

— Joan Hing King, award-winning real estate investor, mentor, and author of The Path to Real Estate Riches.

Money Remixed is a wonderful book that explores how two entrepreneurs built successful businesses. It weaves together personal stories, including one author's background in music, with practical advice on developing what they term a 'wealthy mindset.' Their approach combines positive thinking, gaining insights from failure, holistic wellness, and business strategy. The authors provide a detailed framework to help readers achieve their own entrepreneurial goals.

— Puneet Kuthiala, Best Selling Author

Money Remixed is a game-changer—a powerful blueprint for transforming your mindset and unlocking true financial freedom. Wilkinson and Grant deliver wisdom that inspires action and lasting success. A must-read for anyone ready to thrive!

— Mike Radoor,
International Best-Selling Author of Above Average,
Coach and Serial Entrepreneur

This book is a game-changer. It takes complex concepts and makes them simple, actionable, and inspiring. I've read plenty of self-help books, but Money Remixed stands out with its blend of real-world advice and deep, personal insight. It's a must-read for anyone serious about achieving financial and personal success.

— Judy O'Beirn, President and CEO of Hasmark Publishing

This book is a must-read for anyone who wants to change the way they think about wealth and take control of their thoughts and actions regarding money. The authors provide practical, actionable ways to transform your relationship with money that is aligned with your purpose, passion, and goals. Living life with intention, honesty, and integrity is at the core of their messaging so that you can have a wealthy mindset.

— Christine O'Shaughnessy,
Award Winning and Best-Selling Author
of Mindful Presence in Leadership

Having known Mark Wilkinson for many years in the music industry and after having reached out to him for advice during some pretty dire financial struggles previously, I was more than happy to take a look at "this thing that might help you",when he reached out to me. I'd been having a bit of a rant on my Facebook wall about "Why people are such idiots?" and "Why is it so hard for them to understand even simple instructions?" Although my chosen language was definitely a lot more colourful than that.

When I received a link to join his '5 Days to Remix Your Life' course, my attention was immediately drawn to a big blue button asking to 'Pay Here.' My heart sank a little. My initial delight at being invited into some secret club by someone I respected and admired immediately turned into thoughts of being fleeced for cash for empty promises of all my dreams coming true. I had a long-standing dislike for money and all the problems that it brought in life, due to (as far as I was aware) my upbringing, so I decided there and then that this definitely wasn't for me. Before I had a chance to think up a reasonable excuse not to join, I received a further message saying, "Don't worry about that payment link, here's a complimentary code". I smiled. "I can do that, for sure," I thought. I often wonder how things would have been so different, had I never received that kind offer?

Long story short, that was my first introduction to Mark's 'new' direction as a Success Coach and to the E-Colours, I was immediately blown away at how my Red Strengths and Potential Limiters were so accurate and how it outlined all the problems I had been facing when communicating with those around me, whether work related or at home.

That initial resistance turned into full commitment; my life turned around completely. I first started joining Mark on everything he did surrounding E-Colours and his Life Remixed book clubs, but I always switched off when talk of money exchanging hands came up. I specifically recall reaching out to Mark when there was a slight lull in his output due to his external work commitments, expressing how much I was missing the interaction and inspiration. I'm still none the wiser how it happened (due to the financial commitment involved) but I am beyond grateful that I eventually did become a coaching client of Mark's and then a certified E-Colours Practitioner.

As a 12-month coaching client of Mark's, he helped me understand myself better and started my journey of self-discovery and improvement. My relationships with everyone around me have improved and there are genuinely way too many things to mention in my life that have turned themselves around (financially, physically, spiritually). A few of note to share I am now 2 years alcohol free, I got back into running marathons, myself and my wife have invested in two further properties in Spain (something I would have NEVER considered before) and my website and graphic design clients continue to flood in, paying rates I never thought achievable! All this from understanding myself, overcoming my limiting beliefs and 'Living With Intention'.

I now reach out to other people when I see their frustrations in order to offer to help them, however, thanks to Mark helping me overcome my dislike for talking about money, I am comfortable charging for my services.

— Andy Ward, Inspire & Be Inspired,
100 Day No Alcohol Challenge,
Vocal Booth Weekender, Vocal Booth Radio.

MONEY
REMIXED

Mark Wilkinson and Paul Grant

Published by
Hasmark Publishing International
www.hasmarkpublishing.com

Permission should be addressed in writing to Mark Wilkinson and Paul Grant at hello@liferemixed.co.uk

Editor: Brad Green brad@hasmarkpublishing.com
Cover Design: Anne Karklins anne@hasmarkpublishing.com
Interior Layout: Amit Dey amit@hasmarkpublishing.com

ISBN 13: 978-1-77482-342-2
ISBN 10: 1-77482-342-X

DEDICATIONS

"All that I am or ever hope to be, I owe to my angel mother."

– Abraham Lincoln, former President of USA

Audrey Joan Mackintosh (20th February 1943 to 30th January 2023). A lovely, caring, kind, and devoted daughter, wife, mother, mother-in-law, and grandmother, who always looked out for those around her. Without your support, I would not be the person I am today. Thank you for the immense support, love, and joy you brought to the world in your own quiet yet caring way. I cherish the memories and the love you shared as a way of honouring your legacy. May your memory continue to bring warmth and comfort to my heart, and may your love and kindness inspire me to pass these qualities on to others. Love you always.

– Paul Grant

"The most precious things you can give to your parents are time, love, and care. Care for your parents with love and respect, for you will only understand their full value when you see their empty chair."

– Unknown

Charles Quentin Wilkinson (RIP) and Gillian Brenda Wilkinson: We all owe a debt of gratitude to our parents for our existence on this planet. I wasn't always the most grateful or a model child (as you may have read in *Life Remixed*). I was certainly a challenging and headstrong son. Yet, no matter what I did, they always loved me. Sometimes they were full of fear and anger, and at other times, joy. There is no doubt in my mind that the post-World War II sea of emotions took a toll on both my parents, and I'm sure that was compounded when I was born. I now see all of this with love, total acceptance, forgiveness, and deep appreciation. I also thank my mum profoundly for teaching me and helping me create my own definition of love. This understanding came from my mother's view of both her sons, mostly after she had calmed down from her initial anger, to be honest. However, no matter what crazy caper I got up to, my mum always accepted me completely. There is nothing more pure in this world than a healthy mother's love, and it is deeply rooted in total acceptance.

– Mark Wilkinson

ACKNOWLEDGEMENTS

"No one who achieves success does so without acknowledging the help of others. The wise and confident acknowledge this help with gratitude."

– Alfred North Whitehead, mathematician and philosopher

"Success is never achieved alone, and it is vital to acknowledge the help of others. A wealthy mindset is essential for achieving great things, and an attitude of gratitude towards all people and all things forms part of a wealthy mindset that, with practice and patience, ultimately leads to money and material riches."

– Mark Wilkinson & Paul Grant

In the tapestry of our lives, we have both been blessed with an abundance of support from individuals who, perhaps unknowingly, have left an indelible mark on our journeys. They may not have realised the magnitude of their impact, but their words, actions, and mere presence have shaped the very essence of who we have become. From fleeting conversations to enduring relationships, every interaction holds the potential for profound transformation. In the symphony of life's encounters, these hidden gems of guidance, advice, and shared experiences have worked in unison to mould and refine us into better versions of ourselves. Every interaction in our lives is like a stone thrown into a pond, creating ripples that spread far beyond our immediate perception. While there are too many interactions to name individually in this book, we would like to express our deepest gratitude to everyone who has helped us along the way. On this spiritual journey as human beings, we must choose to view every interaction with this attitude; it is life-changing and life-defining.

– Paul Grant

To Jean Mackintosh, Paul's grandmother, who was an incredible person; her kindness will always stay with me. She made such a positive impact on my childhood and young adult years.

To Audrey Grant, Paul's mother, whom we miss every day. Her memory lives on forever as an inspiration to all who knew her.

To Kenneth Grant, Paul's father, for always being there and encouraging me to find my own path in life.

To Shirley Grant, Paul's sister, for always believing in me.

To Panee Khamsawat, Paul's wife, you are the most honest, caring, and loving person I know.

To Jack Grant, Paul's son, you bring so much joy to my life. Follow a wealthy mindset, and you will always be content with your life.

To Dean Masters, Paul's business partner and friend, who stirred my interest over two decades ago by encouraging me to take the plunge and start our own companies. You paved the way for me to discover a wealthy mindset.

To Lewis Senior, Paul's esteemed business partner, who is an extraordinary individual. His unwavering dedication to helping others has left an indelible impression on Paul. From the moment they started Equilibria, Paul was struck by his infectious passion and genuine desire to make a positive impact in the lives of those around him.

To Mark Wilkinson, from Paul: Though our interactions may have been limited, I am immensely grateful for the impact you have had. Our discussions, however brief, have served as the catalyst that ignited the spark within me, inspiring our partnership and the creation of this book.

To Paul's remarkable business partners—Chris Blunt, Mike Lavery, Jeff Brown, Laura Senior, David Senior, Chris Cherry, and a heartfelt tribute to the late Dagfinn Tromborg—I extend my deepest gratitude for your unwavering dedication and tireless efforts in building our businesses into the successes they are today. Your collective commitment, expertise, and relentless drive have been the pillars upon which our ventures stand, propelling us forward even in the face of challenges.

I am deeply grateful for the profound impact you've all had on my life. Thank you from the bottom of my heart.

– Paul Grant

To Mark's wife, Emma Wilkinson: Your dedication to me, Frankie, both of our families, and our shared success is truly wonderful. You have supported me on this journey from the beginning, and it must be said, I wouldn't be here without you.

To Mark's mum, Gill Wilkinson: Ever since you took me in as a 39-year-old bankrupt, saving me from possible homelessness, I've made it my mission to ensure you have the best possible life. I hope you know how much I love and appreciate you.

To Mark's dad, Charles Wilkinson: For surviving World War II and, I can only imagine, the PTSD afterwards, for always wanting to be a father, enjoying the birth of your two sons, and always being diligent, hardworking, and teaching us all true empathy.

To Mark's brother, Daniel Wilkinson: For bringing great humour, empathy, and support, and being a solid foundation for the family.

To Mark's gran, Mabel Winnett (RIP): Your wisdom has always impacted me, and I am most grateful that you came into our family as we were growing up, always bringing balance, love, and joy.

To all of Mark's clients and the extremely talented people who have ever decided to work with me in any of my businesses, who have booked me to speak or DJ, or asked me to remix their music or their lives—I am truly grateful.

Indeed, life is a remarkable gift, and it is something to be incredibly grateful for. The vast tapestry of experiences that this world offers us is awe-inspiring. From the breathtaking beauty of wildlife and nature, the vibrant cultures worldwide, every unique person we meet, and the multitude of business opportunities—all of which enrich our lives—every moment presents an opportunity for growth, discovery, and connection.

Thank you.
– Mark Wilkinson

CONTENT

"Wealth is largely the result of habit."

— John Jacob Astor, business magnate

PREFACE

"Nothing great happens, until someone becomes passionate about something."

– O'Reilly Learning Platform

For over two decades, Mark and Paul have been fortunate enough to pursue their passion for making money. While everyone has an opinion and some may view this pursuit as cold or inhumane, let us clarify that it begins with adding value and creating great service, which goes well beyond personal gain. Their true drive stems from a desire to help those around them achieve financial comfort through ethical means. This essentially means making as much money as possible and living a happy, healthy, and wealthy life, without ever harming another human being.

Mark and Paul have witnessed first-hand how a lack of funds can cause immense anxiety and fear among families and individuals alike. With that in mind, it becomes a social responsibility to spread relief by sharing their wealth of knowledge. However, achieving monetary success is actually the final step in the process. The journey begins with self-development and creating a wealthy mindset; the mind must be conditioned to attract and understand the flow of money. Numerous factors must be developed first before achieving overall prosperity.

Paul was initially hesitant about writing a book on money. However, after Mark wrote *Life Remixed* [1], Paul was persuaded otherwise: sharing this important information has the power to inspire others who may not have the knowledge and experience that they both possess.

By following certain steps over the past 20 years—and committing to and creating a wealthy mindset—they have cultivated an approach that has led to a more accomplished life, including financial prosperity. They are now eager to share this approach with others around the world—and Paul extends a heartfelt thank you to Mark for the *Life Remixed* inspiration!

[1] Mark Wilkinson has come from being an international house music DJ and record producer (having been a resident DJ at the world-famous Ministry of Sound in London, playing music in 65 different countries across the world and achieving a UK Top 10 hit!), to now being a multiple business owner, Success Coach, motivational speaker, and international best-selling author - www.markwilkinsonofficial.com/about-mark-wilkinson/

INTRODUCTION

"Great things are not done by one person. They're done
by a team of people."

– Steve Jobs, co-founder of Apple

Why is money such a taboo subject for so many people? The adage, "Don't discuss politics, religion, or money," rings true for many, often because it ends in an argument over the dinner table! However, wealthy people are happy to discuss money. In fact, it's a great subject for them to talk about openly. Why is that? Why isn't everyone taught this?

Mark remembers Bob Proctor educating a group once, saying, "If you teach your children one thing, teach them to earn money—they'll be forever grateful." When Mark heard that, it resonated with him. He had never been taught to earn money; instead, he was told to get good grades, get a job, and work until retirement. That was all he heard growing up from everyone around him. When he read Richard Branson's book, he realised he had been taught entirely differently and had achieved far better results than Mark did up until the age of forty! If you've read *Life Remixed*, you already know this.

So why do the masses avoid talking about money, while the wealthy embrace it? Is it that most people generally don't have it? Or, if they do have money, they never seem to have enough? Why is most of the world's wealth controlled by only a few people? These are fascinating questions that need to be answered.

Mark read many books over the years and studied with some incredibly successful people. He realised that everything starts with our beliefs. Our thoughts and feelings programme our beliefs, which then shape our attitudes. This attitude in turn programmes our habits, which ultimately brings our results. To test his own changes, he started again from bankruptcy after a disease at 39 years old. He was coached and trained to completely change his mindset about money, and now, 14 years later, the results are astounding. He retrained himself to create his own wealthy mindset.

A wealthy mindset refers to a set of beliefs, attitudes, and habits conducive to achieving your purpose in life. It involves adopting a positive and proactive approach towards life, with a focus on adding value to others and backing it up consistently with great service. It's important to note that a wealthy mindset is not solely about accumulating financial wealth but more about how you approach life, with financial wealth being one of the outcomes.

Through a comprehensive exploration of the 14 Steps to a Wealthy Mindset, we will delve into the core principles, strategies, and mindset shifts required to unlock your full potential. Paul started this journey back in 1990, and the results are remarkable. He can truly say he is living a wealthy mindset: providing for his family, spending time with them, having freedom in how he uses his time, being financially independent, continuing to grow his financial wealth, enjoying some guilt-free spending, and loving every minute of this remarkable journey, all while ensuring that he continues to follow his ethics.

After reading *Money Remixed* and putting its principles into practice, you'll be better equipped to navigate life's challenges with your own new wealthy mindset, never allowing other people's thoughts, words, or actions to knock you off course. This will increase your likelihood of turning every situation you encounter into an opportunity. By creating and protecting this mindset, you'll unlock your potential to grow as a person and increase your financial assets to achieve the lifestyle you deserve—for yourself, your loved ones, and everyone around you. Not only will you experience financial growth, but your entire life will flourish with newfound prosperity. Creating money in your life allows you to reach further and impact more people with your own positive message. It is something to be enjoyed and shared—being in the flow of money.

Within the pages of Bob Proctor's enlightening book, *It's Not About the Money,* you will discover that embracing a wealthy mindset brings forth far more than mere financial gain. This captivating read is undoubtedly worth your time and consideration. The audiobook, narrated by Bob himself, is also well worth a listen. Switch off the negative, repetitive 24-hour news, and focus on prosperity and bringing value to the world.

Another interesting read is *Baby Steps Millionaire* by Dave Ramsey, which sets out steps to get yourself on track to achieve millionaire status.

These two books, in conjunction with *Money Remixed*, will get you moving in the right direction.

The 14 Steps to a Wealthy Mindset

In both Mark and Paul's separate journeys to a wealthy mindset, they have come to realise that cultivating a rich and fulfilling life begins in the mind. Many people chase money without first addressing this crucial detail. "Love people and use money" is wonderful advice, but unfortunately, many people get these two the wrong way around. Loving money and using people leads to a life of deep unhappiness.

Throughout the past two decades, especially, they have both discovered—through their own trial and error—a set of steps have served as a guiding force, propelling them forward in their pursuit of happiness and prosperity. These steps, which they hold dear, can be summarised as follows:

1. Wealthy mindset people have a clear vision and purpose(s) in mind.
2. Wealthy mindset people concentrate on adding value in every moment.
3. Wealthy mindset people are focused on their goals in life.
4. Wealthy mindset people revise their purpose, vision, and goals as needed.
5. Wealthy mindset people define and use their ethics to guide their daily decisions.
6. Wealthy mindset people take consistent action to have a happy mind and healthy body.

7. Wealthy mindset people create a white-hot desire for success through a positive mindset.

8. Wealthy mindset people consciously surround themselves with other people who possess a wealthy mindset.

9. Wealthy mindset people appreciate and understand the importance of other people and the diversity of thought.

10. Wealthy mindset people manage their time by prioritising and completing tasks.

11. Wealthy mindset people manage their financial wealth.

12. Wealthy mindset people choose faith, confidence, and belief over fear, always.

13. Wealthy mindset people learn from both their successes and failures in life.

14. Wealthy mindset people continue to develop their learning and knowledge each day and are comfortable asking for help from others when needed.

Many people may initially resist these steps towards leading a more accomplished, complete life while becoming financially wealthy, dismissing them as unrealistic or unattainable. However, there are individuals like Mark and Paul who have defied such fear and scepticism and demonstrated that these steps can indeed lead to financial wealth. By embracing inspiration, determination, discipline, and strategic decision-making, they have proven that the path to wealth is not just an impossible dream but a tangible reality. Through their own accomplishments, they challenge those who doubt the feasibility of these steps to reconsider their preconceptions and open their minds to the possibilities that lay within their reach.

Take the time to observe what they share and how they have applied these steps. Then define your own steps that will work for you. We all have unique ways of thinking and acting—our personalities, including how we define our vision, purpose(s), and goals in life. Utilise the foundation they have provided; then shape your steps to reflect your individuality.

Money plays a significant role in our lives. For us to have food, clothing, and shelter, money is a necessity. English statesman Francis Bacon once said, "Money is a great servant but a bad master." Money has the power to enhance your comfort and create wonderful experiences. While money is a natural outcome of a wealthy mindset, it must not be the sole focus of an individual.

Now, let's shift the focus from the authors to you, the readers. It is said that repeating the same actions while expecting different results is a form of insanity. Therefore, when examining the 14 Steps to a Wealthy Mindset, ask yourself these important questions:

- How satisfied are you with your current results?
- Are you willing to embrace change to achieve better outcomes?

Throughout *Money Remixed*, you'll come across various quotes at the beginning of the chapters. We often say to our coaching clients that all these successful people cannot be wrong, and their success leaves clues for us. Take time to study people who are living the way you would like to live and copy them. Take a moment to consider how each of these quotes resonates with the lessons and knowledge you gain from each chapter. If you come across a quote that resonates more deeply with you, jot it down and look at it often. Better still, speak it aloud to reinforce the message. This will help you forge a personal connection with the specific concepts you're learning and decide to take in and practice.

As co-founder of Apple, Steve Jobs, once said, "Great things are not done by one person. They're done by a team of people." Consider this book as a valuable member of your team. Nurture your team, cultivate your wealthy mindset, be patient, and day by day, watch your life flourish and your financial wealth grow alongside it. It works for every person, every time.

Remember, there's a distinction between reading and studying. This book contains many "golden nuggets" that may only reveal themselves upon subsequent readings. Always remember: repetition is mastery. Approach this book as a study guide, focusing on what you can learn rather than simply reading through it and then putting it down. This way, you'll discover a treasure trove of valuable insights that you can apply to your own life.

It really is this simple: money is energy.

Money is attracted to you like anyone or anything else is attracted to you in this life. Money and people are always attracted based on your energy: negative energy pushes good people and good money away from you; positive energy attracts good people and more good money to you. In our experience, it really is that simple, with the lovely added bonus that the positive energy you create makes you feel happy, healthy, and wealthy about people, money, and this wonderful life we all have been blessed with.

Contained in the pages of this book, we will give you every piece of information required for you to create your own wealthy mindset, along with the financial freedom that will ultimately follow as a result. The information we share in these pages is truly a win-win. Get ready to change your financial destiny and remix all the money in your life.

CHAPTER 1

~~~~~

THE YOUNGER YEARS

"The years of early childhood are the time to prepare the soil."

– Rachel Carson, conservationist

Paul John Grant

Born on Sunday, the 17th of November 1968, on an RAF base in Akrotiri, Cyprus, I only called it home for 10 weeks before moving to a new home in the United Kingdom. My sleeping quarters for the flight were in an aircraft storage locker, adapted just for me. My father was serving as part of his 25 years in the RAF. Although I always planned to revisit Cyprus, it remains on my list of places to go—a "not yet done" item that I don't lose much sleep over, but perhaps one day.

The next seven years took me to homes in Auldearn in Scotland, Leuchars in Fife, Scotland, and Grove in England before we finally settled in my mother's home village of Auldearn, Scotland. There, my parents purchased and ran a shop for nine years while my father completed his service in the RAF.

My earliest memories are of playing with a toy robot in my Granny Mackintosh's house in Auldearn. My sister and I would run around the room screaming as the tin toy made noises and spouted sparks from its mouth. Certain toys bring back happy childhood memories. The robot, a pedal tractor, and a World War II rifle powered by caps, were all provided by my grandmother Mackintosh.

During those formative years in Auldearn from 1975 to 1984, my grandmother Mackintosh, my mother, and my father profoundly influenced my development. Respect for elders, lending a helping hand to those in need, delivering groceries, taking out the bins, chopping wood, doing the garden, or delivering papers—earning pocket money through hard work—these were the values instilled in our household. It was during these early years that I developed a passion for earning money and the freedom it provided. The soil was certainly being prepared for my future life.

It's interesting how we often pass on the same values to our children that we were taught as kids. As the father of a nine-year-old son now, I realise the importance of the ethics that shaped me. Respecting people, keeping promises, being honest, helping others, understanding different perspectives, practising forgiveness, expressing gratitude, managing finances, and striving for success while enjoying life—these are the principles I learned as a child and continue to follow today.

Auldearn Primary School provided an excellent learning environment, and the headmaster, Mr. Patrick Lobban, was a highly respected figure in our community. I have priceless memories of summer camps in Nethy Bridge, winter skiing trips in Aviemore, and visits to Italy and Switzerland—so much fun and laughter. The school's efforts, along with my parents' support in funding these adventures, made for a truly happy childhood.

Transitioning to Nairn Academy School, a ten-minute bus ride away, only added to the joyful memories. I played rugby during breaks from my job delivering newspapers and groceries from my parents' shop. I also found time for indoor and outdoor bowls, schoolwork, and hanging out with my friends. Those six years flew by.

When I turned 15, my parents sold the shop in Auldearn and purchased a hotel in Nairn called The Millford Hotel. It was there that I saw an opportunity to pursue my passion for becoming an engineer and earning a substantial income. The hotel became a temporary home for several subcontractors employed at the Ardersier oil rig construction site. These individuals had a significant influence on the career path I would eventually choose. Claude, one of the project managers, and David, one of the engineers, often took me to the construction yard and showed me the massive oil rigs. They shared stories of their exciting jobs around the world, highlighting the travel opportunities and comfortable lifestyle available to engineers.

While at Nairn Academy, I remember selecting subjects that would enable me to attend Heriot-Watt University in Edinburgh and pursue my dream of becoming an engineer. After meeting the required entry qualifications, I embarked on four incredible years of studying civil engineering. I finished third in my class, graduating with a First-Class Honours Degree. I still keep in touch with some of my friends from those days through Facebook, witnessing how they have pursued their own careers and are now scattered across the globe—UK, New Zealand, Dubai, and America. The world has indeed become a smaller place in the past few decades, with the advent of cheaper airline travel and communication tools like the Internet, Facebook, LinkedIn, Instagram, TikTok, FaceTime, and WhatsApp. In Chapter 2, I will elaborate on my career in the oil industry and reflect on the limitations of communication in the early 1990s when I worked in the North Sea. For the Gen Z generation, it's hard to imagine a time when sending and receiving letters during a two-week offshore shift was the primary means of communication with your family. I am somewhat envious of Gen Z, who grew up in an era where more advanced communication technology came naturally as part of their learning. That being said, I would not swap my younger years for anything—I had a blast.

During my time in Edinburgh, I experienced considerable stress during exams. Recognising my distress, my parents sat me down and said, "If you're unhappy with what you're doing, make a change. If you want to return and run the hotel, we will all support you, and it won't diminish our opinion of you." Suddenly, the weight on my shoulders lifted, and I found the encouragement I needed to persevere. It wasn't that I didn't want to work with my parents; I simply understood that alternatives existed in life and that I had the power to choose my own path. I will always appreciate this valuable lesson that my parents taught me. When I look at my son Jack, I will strive to be as supportive as my parents were to me, allowing him to forge his own path and offering unwavering support for his decisions.

Mark Wilkinson

I was born on the 3rd day of September 1970. As I was growing up, Mum often shared with me that it was the same day World War II broke out back in 1939. I didn't know it at the time, but the aftermath of WWII would deeply affect my family. I wrote about this in *Life Remixed*, so it may well be worth going back and learning about my, and your own childhood, understanding more about your family and your upbringing as the impact of these early formative years on all of us is clear to me today. Limiting beliefs on money can start at a very young age.

As much as they loved me, and I loved them, my early memories of family life were challenging for me. I didn't understand why at the time, but I remember being told that life was difficult, that we had to be fearful, that the world was a scary place, and that we didn't have enough of anything. Usually, these worries revolved around money and the lack thereof.

My mum lived 100% for her boys. She worked so hard for Dan and me. My dad didn't earn enough money to support us all, so sometimes she'd work two or three jobs at a time just to make ends meet. She even took a cleaning job for a while, which I know she disliked immensely. Bless him, my dad was highly intelligent but didn't have enough confidence in himself to earn more, which meant my mum worked her butt off to look after us. As a young man, I saw my mum as strong and my dad as weak. Both observations, as it turns out, were incorrect. They were just good people doing their best with what they had in the 1970s and '80s.

Despite their very best efforts, I was being raised in an environment of a 'scarcity mindset,' and although I didn't know why at the time, I didn't like the feeling. As far as my parents could see, we never had enough of anything. Money was always tight, and I always remember the fear that someone might break in, and we'd be robbed. The notion that we might lose the house for some reason was also a recurring issue. It was a lot of fear and lack for a young lad to deal with.

It clearly didn't help that, from an early age, I was always very demanding and headstrong. Perhaps this was as a result of, and a rebellion towards, my upbringing and environment.

As I grew into a teenager, I found it *all increasingly difficult* to deal with. You've heard of fight or flight, right? Well, with the benefit of hindsight, much of what happened over the next 25 years of my life was my flight mechanism kicking in—escapism of the highest order. I wrote about this in detail in *Life Remixed*.

I ended up leaving school at 16 without much direction and with only a couple of O-levels to my name. I knew I didn't want to carry on studying at school or go on to college. I wanted to get out there, earn my own money, gain my own freedom, and continue the adventure I'd started in the world. But I had no idea what to do jobwise. Mum said, "Get a job in a bank—you'll get decent mortgage rates." I didn't have a better idea, so I strolled into the interview and accidentally got a job working in a bank in Twickenham. Within six months, I was promoted to a team leader and was quickly on my way to a management trainee course.

Similar to my time in school, I made some good friends in the bank, but I knew fairly quickly that I didn't want to stay working there for the rest of my life. It was a real-life comedy moment when I handed in my notice, exactly like the Ricky Gervais as David Brent sketch from *The Office* when Tim wants to leave Wernham Hogg. I had one of the bank's bosses trying to convince me to stay. I was 18, and he was in his mid-thirties. Bless him, he was overweight, bald, and had a bit of a case of halitosis when he sat opposite me and came out with the classic line, "Mark, I don't think you should leave the bank. You have so much potential. In ten years' time—let's be honest—you could be me sitting in the hot seat." Hmm. Let me think about that for a moment. No thank you. It really wasn't for me.

My love of music began around age six and continued to grow, and I always got into venues easily because I was tall; I was an '80s soul boy. However, the '80s Hip-Hop Jams became quite dangerous for a tall, glasses-wearing white kid from the suburbs, and we got robbed more than once. I remember once having to run down Charing Cross Road away from the Astoria Theatre on a Sunday afternoon after we tried to get into a Time Radio Jam (party), and we got jumped (attacked) in the street by a gang just for our tickets!

A couple of years later though, in 1988, I went back to the Astoria for a Saturday night out and walked straight into a room full of people dancing, smiling, sweating, and cuddling each other. It's no wonder I became hooked on that positive energy—everyone dancing to the four-to-the-floor drum beat of house music in Central London. Right then and there, I had landed in the middle of the Summer of Love in London, and the *Life Remixed* journey began.

My issues and fears around money continued throughout my young life. I never earned a huge amount from music, just enough to get by and support some of my poor choices in life. As I learned later, this was in large part due to my low self-esteem and poor self-image, neither of which were particularly good things to believe about yourself, and they both needed a lot of therapy and then life coaching to let go of!

As it turned out, these pre-programmed, subconscious fears that I held onto from childhood for many years were a big part of my downfall in my '30s; the fear of ill health and the fear of poverty came home to roost when my health failed me and I lost all my money and possessions. Thankfully, I still had time to rebuild, and that is what *Life Remixed* and *Money Remixed* are all about.

CHAPTER 2

EARLY CAREERS

*"By working faithfully eight hours a day you may
eventually get to be boss and work twelve hours a day."*

— Robert Frost, poet

Paul John Grant

It was 1989, and as the final exams loomed, so did the pressure of choosing a more defined career path as an engineer. The job market appeared ripe with opportunities for young engineers, and the prospect of entering the workforce was both exciting and intimidating. With an honours degree in civil engineering within reach, I found myself torn between staying on the familiar path within the construction industry or venturing into the oil and gas sector.

The allure of success stories lingered in my mind, impossible to ignore. Tales of triumph and achievement, particularly those of David and Claude, who had carved out remarkable careers in oil and gas, echoed in my thoughts. Their journeys had been nothing short of inspiring, marked not only by a deep sense of purpose but also by the substantial financial rewards that came with their work.

As graduation approached, I stood at a critical crossroads, contemplating the numerous paths before me. It was a moment of transition and transformation—a juncture where the possibilities felt both overwhelming and exhilarating.

The demand for engineers was evident as I navigated a whirlwind of job interviews. The competitive landscape unfolded before me, with ten interviews resulting in nine tempting job offers—each a testament to the industry's insatiable appetite for talented individuals. The abundance of opportunities required careful thought and introspection.

Among these offers, two names stood out, carrying an undeniable prestige. The oil and gas industry, with its vast potential, called to me through opportunities with BP and Schlumberger. These industry giants held a commanding presence, their financial prowess and market capitalisation impossible to overlook.

BP, with its staggering 2022 revenues of USD 241 billion, embodied the essence of a formidable force in the sector. Its name carried weight and significance, symbolising both financial stability and global reach. Schlumberger, with its 2022 revenues of USD 28.09 billion, stood as a powerhouse in its own right, respected and admired within the industry.

As I considered these options, the names BP and Schlumberger whispered promises of growth, learning, and professional fulfilment. Their stature in the industry beckoned, inviting me to become part of their extraordinary legacies. With their substantial resources, unwavering dedication, and global influence, they epitomised the very essence of the oil and gas sector.

After much deliberation, I found myself facing a pivotal decision—one that would shape the trajectory of my career. Financial factors weighed heavily on my mind, as did the allure of global adventure. BP, despite offering a lower salary than Schlumberger, presented an opportunity that far exceeded the financial prospects of the civil engineering roles before me, coupled with the attractive prospect of international travel.

With a mix of excitement and apprehension, I ultimately chose BP, driven by the promise of a career that included the potential for global exploration. Little did I realise at the time the profound impact this decision would have on my journey into the oilfield.

Fate, however, had more in store for me, as my path would soon intersect with Schlumberger in unexpected ways, leading to unforeseen opportunities and collaborations. Within two short years, my professional journey would intertwine with Schlumberger, revealing a shared destiny within the oil industry.

Life in the oilfield pulses with a different rhythm. The air crackles with anticipation as the rig comes alive under the vast expanse of the open sky. It's a world where hard work and determination mix with the hum of machinery and the distinct smell of oil and mud. From the moment you step onto the rig, you become part of a close-knit community, united by a common purpose—to harness the energy that powers our modern world. Days blur into nights as the relentless pursuit of black gold becomes a way of life. It's a career that demands resilience, courage, and an unyielding spirit, but it also opens doors to camaraderie, adventure, and the satisfaction of being at the forefront of a global industry.

With a First-Class Honours Degree secured, the much-coveted job with BP was finally within my grasp. The anticipation was palpable as I joined a select group at the Aberdeen Training Centre. Sarah, Joe, Pete, and Hank—my fellow trainees—had also been chosen to embark on BP's drilling engineering graduate training programme, a comprehensive two-year journey blending classroom learning with hands-on experience.

The programme promised to be an adventure like no other. We were immersed in a diverse range of topics, from offshore survival and firefighting to drilling practices, well control, and subsea operations. Our minds absorbed the knowledge while our spirits soared with the excitement of what lay ahead. The training was a perfect mix of rigorous instruction and practical applications, equipping us with the skills needed to thrive in the challenging world of drilling engineering.

For two weeks at a time, we found ourselves offshore, working on the imposing Sedco 711 or John Shaw semisubmersible rigs, or on the Clyde, Magnus, or Thistle platforms. The offshore life became our temporary home, and we embraced it with enthusiasm. We faced the elements head-on, tackling the complexities of drilling and completion operations while forging deep bonds of camaraderie. The long shifts were rewarded with moments of respite, where we soaked in the stunning vistas of the open sea, cherishing the solitude amidst the constant hum of machinery.

After our offshore stints, we would have a few days of rest, savouring the brief downtime before diving into the next phase of training. Whether it was a week-long course or a few days assisting in office projects, the learning continued. And amidst the intensity, we always found time for socialising and unwinding. The bars of Aberdeen and wherever our training took us became our sanctuaries, where we celebrated milestones, swapped stories, and perhaps spent a little too much of our hard-earned salaries.

As the programme progressed, we became more than colleagues—a tight-knit group of friends forged through the unique challenges and experiences of the oilfield. Little did we know that the real test of our abilities awaited us beyond the shores of the UK, as our careers would take us to far-flung locations, presenting us with new trials and triumphs that would shape us in ways we couldn't yet imagine.

As our training programme neared its conclusion, the time came for us to venture beyond the familiar confines of the UK and embrace the challenges of working in new and unfamiliar territories. First on the horizon was a three-month assignment in Yemen, a land of mystery and intrigue.

With my passport stamped and adrenaline coursing through my veins, I embarked on the journey to Yemen, eager to apply my skills and knowledge in the Middle East. The vibrant streets, bustling markets, and the aroma of exotic spices greeted us as we acclimated to this captivating country. The work was demanding, but the experience was transformative. I adapted to the local customs, collaborated with local teams, and absorbed the rich cultural tapestry that surrounded us. It was in Yemen that I truly grasped the global reach and impact of the oilfield industry.

Following my time in Yemen, my path led me to the serene landscapes of Wytch Farm in the south of England. Nestled amidst forests and verdant countryside, this oilfield site held its own unique charm. I ventured into land-based operations, witnessing first-hand the intricacies of drilling in an onshore, environmentally friendly setting, where regulations were stringent. From reservoir management to production optimisation, we delved into the complexities of maximising oil extraction from this picturesque location. During our downtime, we explored nearby towns and villages, immersing ourselves in the local heritage and creating lasting memories.

These assignments in Yemen and Wytch Farm pushed me out of my comfort zones, testing my adaptability and resourcefulness. I encountered cultural nuances, navigated logistical challenges, and honed my technical skills amidst diverse landscapes. Through it all, I formed bonds that transcended borders and backgrounds, working alongside others to overcome obstacles and achieve success.

Little did I know that these experiences were just the beginning—stepping stones on a much grander journey. The oilfield, with its ever-evolving landscapes and endless possibilities, beckoned us to explore further and discover what lay beyond the horizon. My career had taken root in the oilfield, and as I looked ahead, I saw it filled with anticipation, ready to embrace the next chapter and all the adventures it held.

Life in the oilfield is full of surprises, and just when I thought my path was firmly set within BP, destiny had other plans.

Schlumberger, a giant in the oilfield services industry, came knocking at my door, offering an opportunity that seemed too good to pass up.

The position they offered was as a rig engineer, working onboard the esteemed Sedco 700 rig—the flagship, as often pointed out by Howard Meredith, OIM—contracted by Shell on the Osprey development. The mere mention of the offer nearly knocked me off my feet. Not only was it a chance to work on a high-profile project, but the prospect of doubling my current salary was simply staggering. It was an offer that made my head spin and my heart race.

Initially, I couldn't believe such an opportunity had come my way. Doubts crept in—was it all too good to be true? Those "what if" scenarios we often talk about as fear began to surface. But after careful consideration, weighing the pros and cons, I made the bold decision to resign from BP and embark on a new chapter with Schlumberger.

Leaving behind familiar faces and the comfort of my previous company wasn't easy, but the allure of this exciting opportunity was impossible to resist. It was a chance to broaden my horizons, push my limits, and explore new frontiers within the oilfield industry.

With a mix of nervousness and anticipation, I stepped onto the Sedco 700 rig, ready to tackle the challenges ahead. Working alongside Shell, I found myself in a dynamic environment where precision and teamwork were paramount. The days were filled with rig operations, troubleshooting, and collaborating with a diverse team of professionals.

The decision to join Schlumberger marked a turning point in my career. It opened doors to new experiences, expanded my skill set, and introduced me to a network of talented individuals from around the world. The oilfield, with its ever-changing landscape, once again proved its capacity to surprise and provide unexpected opportunities for growth.

As I settled into my new role, I couldn't help but reflect on the twists and turns that had brought me to this point. Life in the oilfield was a continuous journey, filled with unexpected detours and thrilling possibilities. I embraced the uncertainty, knowing that every choice would shape my path and contribute to the ever-evolving story of my career in the oilfield.

Life in the oilfield is characterised by its constant change, and my journey aboard the Sedco 700 was no exception. My time on the rig was brief, lasting less than six months before a new challenge emerged, testing my abilities in unexpected ways.

The next chapter of my career called as I was tasked with assisting the Drill Star, another rig contracted to Shell, and later Conoco Philips. This time, my role involved working closely with the team to prepare a safety case—an essential document ensuring adherence to rigorous safety standards, a direct result of the Piper Alpha catastrophe enquiry. The responsibility was immense, but the chance to contribute to the crew's safety and the operation's success filled me with a deep sense of purpose.

As if the challenge of the safety case wasn't enough, an even greater opportunity arose. Don Boser, the rig manager, entrusted me with the role of relief rig manager during his well-deserved time off. The weight of this responsibility was enormous, but I embraced the chance to lead the team, guiding them through the intricacies of rig operations and ensuring the smooth, safe execution of our duties.

These challenges were stepping stones on a path that led me higher and higher. Each hurdle presented a chance for growth and learning. The oilfield had a way of pushing me beyond my comfort zone, revealing strengths and capabilities I hadn't realised I possessed. The fulfilment and accomplishment that accompanied each triumph were unparalleled.

As I reflect on these experiences, I am filled with gratitude for the challenges that came my way and for the support I received from those around me. The oilfield consistently presented opportunities that stretched me, tested me, and ultimately shaped me into the professional I became. These challenges were just the beginning—a prelude to the heights I would reach and the adventures that awaited in my ongoing career.

The oilfield journey continued to offer new challenges and opportunities for growth. As the Drill Star chapter closed, a staff engineer position on the Sedco 714, contracted to Shell, beckoned me towards a new adventure. This role demanded more than just drilling engineering expertise—it required a comprehensive understanding of the entire drilling operation, from directional drilling and measurement while drilling to cementing and fishing.

The Sedco 714 became my stage for this multifaceted endeavour. It was a time of intense dedication and unwavering commitment. Early starts at 6:30 a.m. and late finishes at 8:00 p.m. became the norm. Resilience and perseverance were essential qualities in this environment. Even weekends were not spared, as duties extended to the other rigs within the fleet, numbering around ten in total.

Navigating through this challenging period required a balance of technical expertise, effective communication, and resource management. The Sedco 714 served as a platform for continuous learning and adaptation. Each day brought new lessons, allowing me to refine my skills and broaden my knowledge. The camaraderie within the team, built on trust and a shared sense of purpose, propelled us forward, even during the most demanding times.

But as this chapter closed, yet another opened. This time it was the role of rig manager on my horizon, a goal that had been shaping my aspirations. In May 1995, I achieved this milestone, stepping into the role of rig manager with a mix of excitement and responsibility, overseeing a drilling unit generating over GBP 3,000,000 per month in revenue.

Leading a rig meant shouldering the immense responsibility for the crew's well-being, the successful execution of operations, and adherence to safety protocols. It required a delicate balance of leadership, technical expertise, and a deep understanding of the unique dynamics governing life in the oilfield.

As I embarked on this new phase of my career, I couldn't help but reflect on the journey that had brought me here. The oilfield had been a relentless teacher, pushing me to my limits, moulding me into a resilient and capable professional. The path to rig manager was not easy, but it was one I embraced wholeheartedly.

Following a successful USD 10 million upgrade of the Sedco 714 to a High Pressure High Temperature unit, an exciting new chapter in my career began. In April 1997, I was offered the opportunity to take on an international assignment as Country Manager in Gabon, West Africa. This role would not only broaden my horizons but also test my capabilities. With the responsibility of overseeing five land rigs and an offshore unit, I was about to embark on a major challenge—a transformative journey outside the UK, one that would continue to test my resolve.

Just a year later, in 1998, another opportunity arose. This time, it was an invitation to move to Thailand and assume the position of Country Manager for Thailand and Vietnam operations. It was a remarkable chance to expand my skill set and take on new responsibilities. I would now lead a team managing four jackups and a semisubmersible unit. The prospect of working in a new cultural setting and exploring the potential of these regions filled me with anticipation and excitement.

In the year 2000, a seismic shift occurred within Sedco Forex as it was announced that the company would merge with Transocean, creating the world's largest drilling contractor. This transformative event had profound implications for my career. Suddenly, my plans of staying in Thailand were uprooted, and I found myself being relocated to Houston for a corporate role of great importance. As Director of Compensation & Benefits, I was entrusted with the monumental task of merging the company's compensation packages. This role demanded strategic thinking, meticulous planning, and a keen eye for detail.

By January 2001, the complex process of merging compensation packages was successfully completed, and I was ready for the next chapter of my journey. It was time to take on a new challenge—a fleet of approximately 17 rigs awaited me in Brazil. Tasked with the role of Human Resources Manager, my goal was to bring structure and coherence to this expansive fleet from an HR perspective. Just as I was settling into my role, fate intervened once again. The Vice President of Human Resources unexpectedly resigned, and I was called upon to step into this crucial position for eight months. It was a daunting responsibility, but one I embraced fully. Overcoming numerous obstacles, I successfully navigated the intricacies of HR management and survived several Board meetings. My reward from the CEO and new VP of Human Resources was the chance to choose my next transfer—and I chose Asia.

In September 2001, my journey took me to Indonesia, where I assumed the role of Director of Marketing & Sales for the Middle East and Asia. This new chapter allowed me to explore the vast potential of these regions, capitalising on both existing and emerging markets, and forging valuable partnerships. For nearly three years, I immersed myself in the dynamic landscapes of the Middle East and Asia, steering the marketing organisation towards new heights of success.

These experiences—shaped by mergers, organisational challenges, new business contacts, and international assignments—became the crucible in which my leadership skills were forged. Each opportunity tested my mettle and pushed me beyond my limits. They were simultaneously the most demanding and rewarding tasks I had ever encountered.

However, as I reflected on my journey and the various roles I had undertaken, I began to question whether my career in the drilling industry still ignited the same passion within me. Despite the remarkable opportunities and achievements I had experienced, a lingering feeling tugged at my core. Something seemed to be missing, and I couldn't shake the sense that there was more to life than the corporate path I had been following.

During this introspective period, a conversation with Dean Masters, soon to be a trusted business partner and close friend since 1998, sparked a glimmer of hope. He shared his belief that my extensive knowledge and connections could be utilised in running multiple companies, accumulating wealth, and pursuing other aspirations I held dear. It was a tantalising proposition, one that stirred a deep yearning within me to explore new avenues beyond the confines of corporate life.

I found myself questioning whether a corporate existence truly aligned with my deepest desires and passions. Was it possible that my purpose lay beyond drilling rigs, boardrooms, and corporate structures? The prospect of embarking on a different path, one that allowed me to harness my expertise in unconventional ways and pursue a broader range of dreams, sparked a newfound curiosity.

These questions lingered, fuelling my contemplation and stirring a restless spirit. Deep within, I longed for a connection that resonated with my innermost aspirations. It was a turning point—a moment of introspection and self-discovery that would ultimately shape the trajectory of my future achievements.

Were my 12-hour days about to change?

Mark Wilkinson

In 1989, I found myself dancing in a field to house music. The Summer of Love had rolled on from 1988, and I had bought myself a pair of record decks. Immersing myself in the music scene, I made sure to get involved in everything I could, getting my name out there on the club circuit with my DJ mixtapes. The next natural step was to start 'playing out' as a real DJ to an actual crowd. It began by lugging all my equipment to friends' parties, where I played my tunes. I was a crowd-pleaser, always spinning records that people knew or ones I knew they'd like, and this quickly made me popular.

My first paid gig was nerve-wracking. It was at Reflex in Putney, and I earned £50 for the night. That was soon followed by a mate asking me to become the resident DJ at his new Saturday night event, "Toad in the Hole" at Valbonnes in Maidenhead. Another significant night for my music career development was Sunday's "Shave Yer Tongue" in Bracknell. We ended our weekends in that club every week. The night was named after how your tongue would feel after a weekend of partying—a disgusting analogy, but it was a fantastic party! I loved playing my uplifting tunes there.

I wasn't always the industry favourite, and some other DJs didn't always love me because I was such a crowd-pleaser. I wasn't considered a DJ's DJ, which did bother me a bit since I wanted everyone to love me. However, I did my best not to care, continuing to enjoy seeing people dance to the same tunes that I loved.

One night in Maidenhead, one of the guys from Flying Records in Kensington Market, London, was booked to play at my residency. He loved what I did when I played after him so much that, in the blink of an eye, he got me a job working with him and the rest of the DJ squad at the very cool London record shop. My young man's dream was taking shape.

I had found a way to earn regular money by working in music and nightclubs. I attracted it all without even being fully conscious of what I was doing. Although my gig ratio increased by working in Flying Records with other amazing DJs and record producers, I rarely made any real money from the shop itself because I spent most of my wages on the latest vinyl records. It was like an alcoholic working in a pub. The majority of my living money came from DJing on the weekends.

This was a difficult financial existence. My diary was only booked a few weeks in advance, and there was no feeling of security as such. This was balanced by the amount of fun I was having on those weekends though, but the anxiety during the week was a lot to deal with, and I never really dealt with it properly. I did what I could with the information and skills that I had at the time. However, the feelings of not being enough and not achieving enough really used to bother me.

CHAPTER 3

~~~~~~~~

LIFE BEYOND A CAREER

"If you spend your days doing what you love, it is impossible to fail."

– Ricky Gervais, actor

Paul John Grant

During a challenging week at the Renaissance Hotel in Ho Chi Minh City, Vietnam, in early 2004, I found myself in desperate need of solace and a glimmer of hope. The recent dismissal of a colleague, under what I believed were unjust circumstances, weighed heavily on me. But fate had other plans when I unexpectedly crossed paths with Lewis Senior, a familiar face from our days together in the Houston office. Lewis had always had a knack for bringing light into any situation, and in that moment, he became a beacon of light in my dark world.

As we rekindled our friendship, Lewis quickly sensed the turmoil I was going through. With his usual empathetic smile, he sparked a conversation that would change the course of my life. "We're starting a coaching company," he said, his words brimming with purpose and excitement. "Are you interested?" Normally, I might have brushed off such a suggestion, but our meeting seemed almost destined.

Ever since Dean, another close friend, had encouraged me to pursue my passion for making money, I'd been searching for the next step in my journey. And when Lewis proposed this new venture, it felt as though he had poured gasoline on the fire Dean had lit within me. The timing couldn't have been more perfect.

I was caught between curiosity and uncertainty as I mulled over Lewis's proposition. Was this the opportunity I had been waiting for? Could this coaching company be the vehicle to drive me towards my true potential? As doubts lingered, Lewis's unwavering confidence and belief in our collective abilities began to sway me.

The world seemed to pause as I considered my options. The weight of my past and the potential of the present intertwined, creating a doorway to new possibilities. Gathering my courage, I finally responded, "Yes, Lewis, I'm very interested."

Little did I know that this single decision would set me on a path of inspiration, empowerment, and relentless pursuit of dreams. Together, we would build a legacy that transcended corporate confines, charting a course towards a more fulfilling future.

We embarked on this journey as four visionary founders: Lewis Senior, Dagfinn Tromborg (RIP), John Lake, and myself. It all began on 04/04/04, when our paths converged in John Lake's barn in the tranquil countryside of southern England. During that initial Equilibria meeting, we laid the foundation of our enterprise—its vision: Realising Potential; mission and core values: People FIRST—and mapped out our future. With the wheels now in motion, I made the bold move to resign from Transocean, stepping into a world filled with untapped potential and limitless possibilities. As this book unfolds, readers will witness the birth of a transformative endeavour, driven by the audacity of dreams and my unwavering pursuit of life's true purpose(s).

My initial focus was on shaping a future that extended beyond Equilibria. Recognising Dean's pivotal role in this vision, we forged a strong partnership, agreeing to split everything—responsibilities, risks, and rewards—down the middle. With this commitment, we embraced the unknown, ready to face any challenges that lay ahead. This journey would become a testament to the power of collaboration and the extraordinary heights we can reach when united by a shared dream.

Strategic thinking was crucial as I navigated the complex world of setting up and financing Equilibria from both legal and financial perspectives. My first priority was establishing reliable revenue streams, and the most logical starting point was a consulting agreement with Transocean. Despite their reluctance to let go, this arrangement provided a sense of continuity as I continued offering my marketing expertise as a consultant. This mutually beneficial deal would last a year, providing a vital financial lifeline during Equilibria's early days. Meanwhile, Dean was engaged as a consultant for his own satellite communication company, which was on the verge of being sold. With these two initial revenue streams, we could secure the necessary funds for Equilibria's start-up and ongoing operations, easing the financial strain on our other founding partners. This was strategic financial planning at its finest, turning visionary ideas into reality and laying the groundwork for multiple revenue streams.

Our next step was to uncover additional revenue opportunities within the oil and gas industry. An opportunity arose when Glenn Potter, a well control services expert who had previously worked with Transocean in Jakarta, expressed a desire to explore new ventures. Seizing this chance, Glenn and I met in the atmospheric basement bar of The Park Lane Hotel in Jakarta—now the Wyndham Casablanca Jakarta—to forge an alliance aimed at creating a well control company. This venture would complement Equilibria's coaching services, broadening our scope and providing another revenue stream. Dean and I would be responsible for funding this new venture.

Our entrepreneurial journey was taking shape, fuelled by strategic partnerships and a relentless drive to seize untapped opportunities. Over the next two decades, we explored various strategic ventures that propelled our growth and diversification. These included:

1. Offering administrative expertise to streamline and optimise internal processes, ensuring efficiency and sustainable growth.

2. Crafting comprehensive Health, Safety, and Environment (HSE) manuals, providing essential guidance and compliance solutions for industry clients.

3. Developing a well control manual template, equipping organisations with critical knowledge and protocols to ensure safety and improve operational efficiency.

4. Creating operations manuals to streamline processes and optimise performance across all aspects of our business.

5. Establishing a workshop facility in Singapore, expanding our operational capabilities, and enhancing service delivery.

6. Opening payroll opportunities for small drilling contractors, simplifying financial operations, and reducing administrative burdens for our partners.

7. Continuously offering consulting, contract negotiations, and marketing services to small drilling contractors, helping them enhance market presence, negotiate contracts, and attract lucrative opportunities.

8. Leveraging our extensive human resource expertise to support medium-sized drilling contractors, offering insights and assistance in restructuring HR systems.

9. Venturing into whisky investment, recognising the potential for significant returns, and diversifying our portfolio with a keen eye for opportunity.

10. Investing in properties, capitalising on the real estate market to secure long-term assets and generate returns through rental income.

11. Expanding my financial portfolio by acquiring precious metals, recognising their value as stable and secure investments, while bundling them into a diverse portfolio.

12. Engaging a wealth management expert to manage a portfolio of equities, bonds, and alternative investments.

But we weren't finished yet. Through Dean's connections, we launched a cyber-security company within the marine industry—A9X Cyber Security—addressing the growing complexities and vulnerabilities of the digital age. As technology increasingly integrates with maritime operations, the need for robust cyber-security measures has become critical. From shipping companies to offshore installations, A9X tackles the unique challenges and risks of the marine industry, developing innovative strategies to protect critical infrastructure, sensitive data, and maritime assets from cyber threats.

Within the pages of this book lies a strategic opportunity with the potential to unlock a vast world of untapped potential— not just for me, but for you as well. By embracing its contents, you can uncover numerous avenues for expanding your revenue streams. This book serves as a stepping stone towards future ventures, presenting the possibility of creating specialised courses or securing television rights. Recognising the value within these pages also opens up a world of possibilities for you by following a wealthy mindset. The opportunities that will arise from this book are boundless, providing an ever-expanding horizon for growth and success.

My story is a testament to the boundless potential within entrepreneurship as we carve a path to lasting success and financial prosperity through diverse ventures and a mindset rooted in innovation and calculated risk-taking—a wealthy mindset. In my story, each venture became an additional revenue stream, sustaining Equilibria's growth and allowing me to explore previously untapped opportunities. Through this extraordinary journey, I lived the dream, passionately pursuing financial success while making a meaningful impact on my other purposes in life. I cannot overemphasise the power of adaptability, innovation, and commitment to following one's passion to achieve extraordinary entrepreneurial heights, while also ensuring you remain focused on your other life purpose(s).

In Chapter 6, all the pieces of my remarkable journey will seamlessly come together, revealing the intricate connections between my entrepreneurial endeavours, strategic partnerships, innovative ventures, and unwavering dedication—all part of a wealthy mindset. This chapter will unveil the hidden layers of wisdom and insight that culminate in a holistic understanding of true wealth, transcending financial abundance to encompass fulfilment, purpose, and a profound impact on my life and that of my family. Through this compelling chapter, readers will be guided to unlock the keys to cultivating a wealthy mindset that embraces all aspects of life, paving the way for extraordinary success and enduring fulfilment.

Mark Wilkinson

After the well documented struggles I faced in *Life Remixed*, one of the things I decided on, committed to, and learned to focus on was to commit to becoming the best in the world at what I decided to do. I dedicated my time, mind, money, and continued effort to becoming highly qualified in various disciplines, while still keeping a place in my heart for DJing and music production. Admittedly, music isn't 100% of my life anymore, but it remains special, especially when I hear—or create—a great track.

To break free from the daily grind, there are countless programmes and qualifications that can enhance your ability to provide excellent service to others. More qualifications, when used and acted upon, generally lead to more money. So, look out into the world, and identify what you truly want to achieve, what you enjoy. Strangely, it was only when I had absolutely nothing materially that I made the big decision to truly go for it—to start learning and developing so I could grow. Tony Robbins says you need "desperation or inspiration in order to succeed." I had both, so with nothing material left to my name, I had a choice: simply give up or dust myself off and try again. Thankfully, I chose the latter, and now that I earn a lot more, I'm in a great position to help others remix their lives.

Part of my growth involved truly committing to knowing my E-Colours strengths and managing my potential limitations. I learned that I'm a big-picture guy and not always brilliant at the details. One of my personal development mantras now is, "I am great at the details," and guess what? I've improved in that area—much better than I used to be. However, I'll readily admit there are people who are far better at the details than I am, my wife, Emma, for example, so I'm more than happy to let those talented people handle the details whenever possible.

In my commitment to growth, I took the excellent online Personal Diversity Indicator (PDI) questionnaire with Equilibria, a company founded by, amongst others, Paul Grant and Lewis Senior. The E-Colours self-awareness system they created was originally used in the energy industry to improve safety and productivity on oil rigs, and from my experience, it's second to none in today's market. I'm deeply grateful to Paul, Lewis, and the Equilibria team for devising the E-Colours programme, which showed me the areas of my personality I needed to develop and work on to become a more rounded individual and succeed in both the corporate and business owner environments.

At a time when I was unsure of what to do with my life, discovering my E-Colours was a lightbulb moment. I used Equilibria's coaching material to climb the corporate ladder to a six-figure salary within a few years. I simply focused on the areas within me that E-Colours identified as needing development. The PDI took only 15 minutes, and the results were astonishingly accurate. It revealed that, at the time, I had Yellow/Blue tendencies, indicating a relating socialiser personality style. My Green (logical thinking) was my lowest percentage, so I knew what I had to do. I took numerous exams and earned qualifications that eventually led to me advising directors at some of the UK's largest companies.

If you'd like more information on this excellent system, please visit my HSE Consultancy website: www.hillmontassociates.com or the Equilibria website www.equilibria.com/PDI-home/ and get in touch with me to discuss it further.

One of the most valuable lessons I've learned about being a good team player is allowing others to excel at what they do. When I was younger, I thought I had to do everything myself. I still see others making this common mistake. However, once I realised that I wasn't the best at everything—and most importantly, that I didn't need to be—I was able to step back and let others shine in their areas of expertise. I also studied and learned that every successful person has a power team around them. Find me a successful person, a multimillionaire for instance, and I'll show you the rest of their power team—the people who helped, supported, and benefited alongside them on their journey.

It's also crucial to decide to do great things with the money you earn. I've learned that money is a tool, a form of circulation that allows me to achieve my larger goal—my purpose (or "why," if you prefer)—which is to help people remix and improve their lives in all areas.

Bob Proctor played a massive role in helping me develop my mind and create an attitude of gratitude for everything that's happened in my life. The incurable disease and bankruptcy I wrote about in *Life Remixed* are two things I wouldn't wish on anyone, yet they turned out to be hugely influential and positive in changing the direction of my life. Every negative event has a positive impact too, even if it's harder to see. Just believe it's there, and you'll find it. I now coach people to move past their issues and limiting beliefs to create a great life for themselves and others.

I later met a wonderful woman named Emma on match.com (online dating can work!). Over time, we developed a bond, appreciating and understanding each other's personalities. We're now partners and a great team. However, it's important to note that I had done a lot of work on myself to become the man I wanted to be, in order to attract Emma. Much of this personal development occurred before I met her. Are you constantly improving yourself to attract who and what you want?

When you're in tune with it, the universe aligns. As a birthday present one year, Emma bought me a ticket to see Tony

Robbins live. We went together for the weekend. Tony spoke for three hours, and it was an incredible experience—both inspirational and energising. I signed up on the spot to attend his "Unleash the Power Within (UPW)" event in London, which was another amazing experience. During this four-day inspirational weekend, I also walked over two thousand degrees of hot coals to prove to myself, once again, that by harnessing the power of my mind, anything is possible.

For many years, I had been thinking about and wanting to write *Life Remixed*, but I never seemed to find the time or the method. Even though I was earning great money and was grateful for it, the corporate world was draining all my energy. I was working over 60 hours a week and was absolutely exhausted. Evenings and weekends were mostly a write-off as I slept through them, and to be honest, that wasn't living—it was a struggle, almost a punishment. Anyone who chooses to work that way for a lifetime has my respect and pity in equal measure!

So, I started studying wealth-building strategies. I also hired a coach because I wanted to leave the corporate world and set up multiple income streams. A good coach is driven by helping others achieve their goals.

Although I was earning a great salary, the stress was taking a toll on my energy and body. My knees had swollen to the point where the rheumatologist was draining up to a litre of fluid from each leg and pumping me full of steroids just to keep me moving. Once again, I could hardly walk, and I knew that the root cause was mental stress and some poor dietary choices. It was a painful time for everyone involved. But pain can lead to positive change, and I knew it had to.

Our coach spoke eloquently about good health and how living as an entrepreneur had allowed him to stay healthy throughout his life. I really connected with this because, as a young DJ and record producer, I had always been an entrepreneur. But now, working for someone else in a world I didn't enjoy, I was unhappy and in pain. I had always preferred being my own boss, yet here I was not doing that and struggling with my health again.

I'd always enjoyed being that self-employed music man, so I knew it was time to return to working for myself—only this time, I'd create my success by listening to Bob Proctor, Tony Robbins, and Kevin Green. I would ensure I had multiple businesses and income streams, building a UK property portfolio and wealth strategies. I knew this was the way to grow and be well-equipped to handle any crisis the world might throw at us. And it turns out I was right.

After a hugely challenging couple of years with my knees, I managed to plan my escape from the full-time corporate job, and I'm glad to say I haven't looked back. So, if your job is costing you too much right now, it's time to decide and then act on it. Your mental and physical health is too high a price to pay simply for a paycheque (no matter the amount!).

I've found that doing something that makes you happy not only adds years to your life but, more importantly, adds life to your years. Have a chat with yourself and answer the questions below. Your answers will help guide your future:

- Do you like your job?
- Are you putting up with it because the thought of change fills you with fear?

- Do you feel stuck or believe you have no other option?
- Will your outlook change if you focus on the positives of your current job?
- Is the pay worth the stress?

After I went through that list, I knew what I had to do. Using the wealth strategies I'd learned, I'm happy to say I've now managed to remix and rebuild my life according to plan, creating multiple businesses and income streams. I provide service and add value to each business throughout the day, and as a result, each business pays me at different times of the month and year, allowing me to relax. I can do what I want, when I want, and with whom I want. I get up when I like, work when I like, holiday when I like, and design and choose my work-life balance daily.

I've been fortunate to meet and attract an excellent success team in various areas of development, and I know you can do the same. Thanks to these choices and the wonderful people around me, I've managed to recover once again from an incurable disease and feel much more at ease working for myself—this time without the toxins and toxic habits.

Twice now, I've recovered from disease, so I can categorically say that the impact of stress and poor diet can trigger an autoimmune condition (AS). From my own experience, there's a direct link between mental health and the stress on our immune system, which is why I've had this incurable autoimmune disease flare up on two separate occasions. As soon as I improved my diet and, more importantly, eliminated stress and found ease again, the disease disappeared—twice. I've now made the decision to stay happy and healthy for the rest of my days and to help others do the same in any way I can.

Nowadays, I enjoy building companies and partnerships with great people. I always prefer cooperation over competition. The only person I compete with is myself—to be better than yesterday. I found that the music and DJ world, as well as parts of the corporate world I was in, could be highly competitive. People were always undermining each other, often for no apparent reason. Perhaps they were trying to get ahead, driven by fear and willing to succeed at any cost? You might have some experience with that. Whenever I saw those behaviours, I was reminded of Napoleon Hill's definition of a genius as "someone who can make life pay whatever they desire without hurting another person."

I knew those environments weren't for me, and my body kept giving me stark reminders in my knees. I now have scars from various operations that remind me of the stress I was under. I work smarter now to ensure I never sink back into that state.

If I can make these changes from the lows I've experienced, as described in *Life Remixed*, so can you. Ask yourself: What are you battling with right now? What's causing you the most stress? Can you cope with it? Do you have difficult people in your life? Can you manage them? Do you reach for comfort food, alcohol, or worse when someone makes you feel bad? Is too much sugar or alcohol a problem for you? Do you have a disease in your body? These are critical questions that you need to answer for a long, happy, healthy, and wealthy life.

All of this is about becoming self-aware, finding your passions and also what you're good at, working on improving yourself, creating multiple sources of income streams, committing to Plan A and having a plan B, C, D, E, F, G that all pay you to ensure you can live your best possible life—happy, healthy, wealthy, and free.

You may recall a story I shared in *Life Remixed* about a doctor who suggested my symptoms might improve if I left stressful situations. He clearly understood the impact of stress on the body. And he was right.

I recovered once before from disease and ran four marathons. The same thing happened when I left the corporate world to start working for myself again.

So now, in addition to being a Success Coach, sharing knowledge and inspiration to help people realise their purpose, life goals, and business ideas, I'm also an E-Colours coach, helping companies improve safety, productivity, team building, one-on-one leadership coaching, and training business development teams to boost their numbers. I now live my own life on purpose.

My key advice on money is that you are the master; money is merely the servant to help you achieve your freedom. Take responsibility, add value, provide great service, and get in the flow, and you'll always be wealthy wherever you are in the world. If I were you, I'd also book and attend one of our upcoming seminars, discover your E-Colours, and get a coach.

HERE'S A FEW REMIX OPPORTUNITIES FOR YOU:

- Be the best version of yourself.
- Money makes us more of what we already are.

- Money is the servant, and you are the master.
- Money is the tool, and freedom is the goal.
- Give service and add value.
- Provide more and better service, adding value to more people, and your income will improve.
- Create multiple sources of income.
- Create your own economy.
- Attend our next "Life Remixed™ or *Money Remixed* seminar.
- Success leaves clues.
- Find someone who is living the way you would like to live and copy them.
- Invest in yourself; it is the ultimate self-love.

CHAPTER 4

~~~~~~~

PERSONALITY DIVERSITY - THE STARTING POINT

"Know Thyself"

– Socrates

"Knowing yourself is the beginning of all wisdom"

– Aristotle

"Be yourself; everyone else is already taken."

– Oscar Wilde, poet and playwright

By acknowledging and embracing the multifaceted nature of personality diversity, we unlock doors to endless possibilities. Appreciating and harnessing the diverse perspectives, skills, and experiences of all people creates an environment where innovation thrives, creativity blossoms, and success becomes not only attainable but also sustainable.

Many years ago, as Mark began his Life Remixed™ journey, a good friend who worked in the offshore energy industry noticed the changes Mark was experiencing and sharing. The friend explained something they used on the rigs called E-Colours Personality Diversity. This system focused on health and safety, as well as the psychology behind accidents. The main question being asked was, "How can I get hurt?"

The first time Mark completed Equilibria's Personality Diversity Indicator online questionnaire, his report revealed Yellow/Blue tendencies. It stated that he loved life and people, enjoyed parties, and was likely musically oriented—all of which, if you've read *Life Remixed*, are 100% accurate. The report also warned that his personality style might lead him to get hurt or even killed by jumping in to help others without pausing to think. Reflecting on his earlier life, Mark realised that he had indeed been doing just that, both mentally and physically, and had suffered as a result.

At the time, this revelation was profound and continues to be so.

So profound, in fact, that Mark immediately sent a message to Lewis Senior, one of the founders via LinkedIn. Lewis duly responded, and a meeting was set in Heathrow Terminal 3. From there, Mark took every opportunity to meet Lewis, which led to a meeting with Paul Grant and his business partner in Asia, some 12 years ago. Mark knew what he wanted in life: to work with people, to help them grow and understand themselves, and to be a worldwide coach.

In traditional Chinese philosophy and astrology, there is a system that associates the four elements—fire, water, earth, and wind—with different personality styles. These elements are believed to influence individuals' temperaments, behaviours, and characteristics.

1. **Fire (Huo)**: The Fire element represents passion, enthusiasm, and assertiveness. People with a Fire personality style tend to be energetic, ambitious, and charismatic. They have a natural ability to inspire and motivate others. Fire individuals are often driven by their desires and are not afraid to take risks. They can be outgoing, adventurous, and have a strong presence in social settings.

2. **Water (Shui)**: The Water element embodies introspection, adaptability, and intuition. Those with a Water personality style are often calm, sensitive, and compassionate. They possess deep emotional intelligence and are skilled at navigating complex situations. Water individuals tend to be imaginative and creative, with a strong sense of empathy and understanding towards others.

3. **Earth (Tu)**: The Earth element represents stability, practicality, and reliability. Individuals with an Earth personality style are down-to-earth, nurturing, and dependable. They have a grounded approach to life and excel in creating harmonious environments. Earth individuals are often patient, loyal, and possess a strong sense of responsibility. They value security, family, and community.

4. **Wind (Feng)**: The Wind element symbolises flexibility, communication, and intellectual agility. Those with a Wind personality style are quick-thinking, adaptable, and have a natural curiosity for knowledge. They possess excellent communication skills and are adept at networking and building

connections. Wind individuals are often open-minded, innovative, and have a love of intellectual pursuits.

These four elemental personality styles offer a framework for understanding the diverse traits and behaviours within individuals. While everyone has a unique combination of these elements, the Chinese belief in their influence provides insights into how different elemental energies shape our personalities and interactions with the world.

Personality diversity is inherent in all individuals. Each person possesses a unique combination of traits, preferences, and behavioural patterns that contribute to their personality. Here are a few key points about personality diversity and how it's currently used:

1. **Individuality**: Personality diversity acknowledges that every person is different and possesses a distinct set of traits and characteristics. No two individuals are exactly alike in terms of their personalities.

2. **The Equilibria E-Colours**: The Personality Diversity Indicator (PDI) is a framework that categorises four main styles: Doer (Red), Socialiser (Yellow), Relator (Blue), and Thinker (Green). The Equilibria system is very well researched, has a strong set of ethics, and is a modern take on personality diversity.

3. **Myers-Briggs Type Indicator (MBTI)**: The Myers-Briggs Type Indicator is a popular framework that categorises individuals into four different personality categories: Extraversion (E) vs. Introversion (I); Sensing (S) vs. Intuition (N); Thinking (T) vs. Feeling (F); and Judging (J) vs. Perceiving (P). This

framework highlights the diverse ways in which people perceive and interact with the world.

4. **The Big Five Personality Traits**: Another widely recognised framework is the Big Five personality traits, also known as the Five-Factor Model. It includes five dimensions of personality: Openness to Experience, Conscientiousness, Extraversion, Agreeableness, and Neuroticism. Each person falls on a continuum for each trait, resulting in a wide range of personality expressions.

5. **Strengths and Weaknesses**: Personality diversity encompasses the strengths and weaknesses of individuals. Different personalities excel in different areas, and recognising and leveraging these strengths can lead to more effective teamwork and collaboration. Equilibria and the E-Colours take "weaknesses" one step further by describing them as "potential limiters." The reasoning behind this is that with a "weakness," you are helpless and stuck with it. However, with a "potential limiter," once you understand, observe, and appreciate it about yourself, you can choose to do something about it—generally through education, training, self-development, and coaching.

6. **Communication and Interaction Styles**: Personality diversity influences how individuals communicate and interact with others. Some people may be more assertive and direct, while others may be more diplomatic and considerate. Understanding these differences can improve communication and foster harmonious relationships.

7. **Career Preferences**: Personality diversity also plays a role in shaping individuals' career choices and preferences. Some

personality styles may gravitate towards careers that require creativity and innovation, while others may prefer structured and organised environments.

It is crucial to appreciate and respect personality diversity in everyone. Embracing this diversity can lead to a more inclusive and supportive environment where individuals can thrive based on their unique strengths and perspectives. It also encourages empathy and understanding, promoting positive interactions and relationships among people with different personalities.

Personality Diversity is the starting point in *Life Remixed* Success Coaching and is one of those golden nuggets that truly transforms our clients' perspectives. We strongly encourage you to visit the Equilibria website and delve deeper into the concept of personality diversity and personal intervention. By taking advantage of the free PDI—Personality Diversity Indicator—you will gain valuable insights into your own personality traits and those of others around you. We advise that you upgrade to a Premium Report using the code MONEYREMIXEDPREMIUM to receive an amazing personalised 33-page E-Colours report about your personality style. The information contained within it has been developed over the last 20 years and will astonish you with how predictable certain personality traits are. This information will act as a multiplier when applying the 14 Steps to a Wealthy Mindset contained in the pages of this book. Remember, there is no right or wrong personality, no better or worse. You are who you are, and we all bring different strengths and values to the table. Embrace personality diversity, and it will help you grow faster than you might otherwise.

Discover Your E-Colours (for FREE): www.equilibria.com/
PDI-home

E-Colours & Personal Intervention: www.equilibria.
com/e-colors

As mentioned earlier, the first time Mark completed his Personality Diversity Indicator, the report was incredibly accurate. The initial E-Colours report showed Yellow/Blue tendencies (though, over years of self-development, he has shifted a few percentages to Yellow/Red). Mark recalls thinking, "Wow! This is amazing, and there are only 12 E-Colour personality combinations for 8 billion people on the planet—how does that work?" Mark decided he needed to know more about E-Colours, and 12 years later, Paul and Mark are now working together on Equilibria and co-authors of this book.

In a simple way, Mark knew that E-Colours taught him two things immediately: First, that it is OK to be himself, as many others also share his personality style. And secondly, it taught him that many people are not like him— and they aren't being intentionally difficult; they just see the world differently. So, he decided he'd better learn how to understand and communicate with them. Understanding this information gives us all the freedom to be ourselves and to understand and appreciate others, leading to the fast track to success and the realisation of potential.

Personality diversity is not merely an abstract concept; it is a dynamic force that shapes our interactions, decision-making processes, and overall success. E-Colours Personality Diversity also distinguishes between personality and character, as these are two very different things we will discuss as we progress through this book.

There is a well-known "golden rule" in life: Treat people as you would like to be treated. While this is a wonderful concept, when we consider the 12 different personality styles in Equilibria's system, or even just the four primary colours, we see an even more important "platinum rule"—Treat people as they *want, need, or would like* to be treated. Doing so will bring out the best in others. After all, if you could become a millionaire on your own, you'd already be one. So, you're going to need others to be on the journey with you, and you'd best know how to understand, communicate with, and inspire them, too.

As we move further into this book, we will explore more on how to harness this knowledge and diversity and apply it in practical ways as part of the steps to earning all the money you desire through a wealthy mindset.

About the authors' E-Colours: Paul's personality traits are Red/Green—the Thinking/Doer. Mark's are Yellow/Red—the Doing/Socialiser (having originally been Yellow/Blue—the Relating/Socialiser). As you'll come to understand, we all have the four E-Colours within us: Red (Doer), Blue (Relator), Yellow (Socialiser), and Green (Thinker). However, some colours are more dominant than others, meaning that by managing our E-Colour tendencies, we can be effective communicators and co-authors. Paul will naturally be direct and to the point, focusing on detail and tasks. Mark will naturally get things done, show empathy, and share stories that emphasise the points being made.

CHAPTER 5

~~~~~~~~~~~

THE CHICKEN OR THE EGG - DIFFERENT PERSPECTIVES

"Appreciating each other's viewpoints and creating success for all"

– Equilibria

In the upcoming steps one and two, we will explore Vision and Purpose(s), and together, we'll tackle the age-old question of what comes first, the chicken or the egg. There is no definitive answer to this question, only different viewpoints on how to achieve success. From the authors' experiences, they each see slightly differing answers, but both agree that Vision and Purpose(s) are equally important steps in developing a wealthy mindset. So, don't fret or overthink the order; the key is to remember that both are crucial and must be addressed on your journey to a wealthy mindset. The sequence can be influenced by both historical learnings and personality diversity.

Let's first look at personality diversity as one of the driving factors:

The Yellow-Socialiser focuses on WHO is involved.
The Red-Doer associates with WHAT is immediately needed.
The Blue-Relator likes to know WHY things are being done.
The Green-Thinker needs to understand HOW things will get done.

Vision is about a future-oriented goal or aspiration, while purpose(s) is about the fundamental reason for existence or action. In essence, for a Red/Green (Thinking Doer), vision provides the WHAT of the future state one wants to achieve or create, while purpose(s) provides the fundamental HOW that motivates and guides actions. They are complementary concepts often used together to provide clarity and direction in personal and organisational endeavours.

– Paul Grant

Purpose is the WHO & WHY, often something that Yellow & Blue E-Colour personalities prioritise. Vision is the WHAT with Goals. The WHEN and the HOW will become clear as the journey continues.

– Mark Wilkinson

Different personality styles will initially focus on what they perceive as important. Both approaches will get you where you want to be, just via different routes.

So, discover your own E-Colours, and decide what works for you in terms of the order in which you define your Vision and

Purpose(s). The important thing is that both are clearly defined and make sense to you.

From Mark's learnings with Bob Proctor and his top-colour Yellow/Blue perspective, Purpose had to be realised first, followed by Vision and Goals. Success only came for him by making sense of things in that order.

While being coached, Mark was continually challenged with questions like, "What is your purpose in life?" and "Why do you do what you do?" His initial response was often, "I don't know! I play records and people dance, that's it!"

From Bob Proctor's 60-plus years of studying Napoleon Hill's self-development classic *Think and Grow Rich* and his constant presence in Mark's life during the *Life Remixed* years, Mark grasped the importance of having a purpose in life and began studying his "Why?" This was not an easy process; it required long and patient effort, starting with self-control, then self-awareness, and finally self-analysis. After much soul-searching, it became clear to Mark that he had already been living his purpose for over 20 years as a DJ and music man (as detailed in *Life Remixed*). At the time, it seemed almost accidental, but by learning more about the Law of Attraction and the Life Remixed™ process, it all began to make sense. Mark had already been living his purpose: to bring joy to others, using music as the tool to reach and uplift people.

More coaching and reflection led Mark to two more insights:

1. Bringing joy is wonderful, but what else could he offer people?

2. If he could use music to bring joy, what else could he do to foster joy in others?

Answering these two questions began to shape Mark's purpose, vision, and goals as he moved forward in his life.

Being a top E-Colour Yellow, fast-paced and big-picture-oriented, and disliking too much detail, Mark embarked on further developing his 'big-picture' purpose. He knew he already enjoyed music, reading, listening, studying, and gaining knowledge. He was also learning that he loved inspiring others and creating things, like books and music. By merging these ideas, Mark defined his life's purpose as: "To bring joy and knowledge, to inspire and create, so that others can learn to live, love, and enjoy their lives to the fullest."

With this clarity in mind, Mark set out to continue his life remix to fulfil this purpose, using any tools that aligned with his purpose and ethics, such as property (providing shelter for others to be happy and secure), music (bringing joy through DJing and producing), books (sharing knowledge to help others), coaching (as a top-colour Yellow, he loves helping others), public speaking (overcoming fear and helping once again), and, of course, money (using it wisely and correctly to bring joy to as many people as possible).

The power of a vision became clear to Mark through a profound experience.

One day in 2004, while on a detox in Scotland, Mark began to understand the power of the vision we possess in our marvellous minds.

At the time, as documented in *Life Remixed*, he was 33, and his body was so stiff with a rheumatic condition that for the previous 18 months, he could barely walk or get up from a chair. He was in so much pain that he had even contemplated suicide.

Brian Miller, an early mentor of his, was with him that day in Scotland. Brian kept challenging Mark to get up out of a chair, to stand up. He raised his voice, urging him to do it, pushing him to get up, get up, get up, stand up, but Mark was in agony and struggling to do so. Finally, Brian relented, asking him to stop trying and to stay seated.

Brian then asked Mark to close his eyes and imagine himself getting up out of the chair—imagine being completely pain-free, walking normally, feeling fit, strong, happy, smiling, and enjoying life.

Mark sat there, struggling at first to clear his mind, but eventually, he managed to focus and do it. Once he had a clear image of himself in his mind, Brian asked Mark to physically begin pushing himself up out of the chair. Slowly, Mark did it and stood there in front of Brian, his body still shaking and very weak.

As Mark stood there, Brian asked him one simple question: "What are you wearing? In your vision, in your imagination, when you are fit, strong, and healthy, what are you wearing?" Mark answered, "A yellow t-shirt." Brian smiled. He knew he had anchored Mark to something, but at the time, Mark didn't think much of it. A quote we've heard since is, "The imagination is the greatest nation on earth."

Fast forward to April 2009. Mark had embarked on a five-year process of detoxing himself completely, avoiding alcohol and other toxins, leaving the past DJ life behind, and cleaning up his thoughts, feelings, and actions to live a better life.

A friend asked Mark, "Would you like to run the London Marathon with me?" Mark trained for four months, going from being unable to walk to running a marathon within a year! Training was tough, but he knew everything he wanted and needed was waiting for him when he crossed the finish line on that warm spring day in Central London.

This is the power of a vision. A few days later, Mark received the official picture of himself happily holding his medal, standing at the end of the 2009 London Marathon. He was smiling, looking fit, strong, healthy—and wearing a bright yellow t-shirt!

There it was, right in front of his eyes. His visualisation from a few years earlier, when he was in real pain and inner turmoil, had actually come true!

Mark found inner peace running the London Marathon—the deep breathing, the almost meditative state of the training, the joy, love, and support, the giving to charity. All Mark could think was, "Wow, this stuff really does work. This is amazing."

Mark called Brian immediately to share the revelation with him. A man of few words, Brian simply said, "Now you know it works."

Looking back, Mark realises this is how he became the resident DJ at the Ministry of Sound in 1996—he had visualised the whole thing while standing on the dancefloor of that great club.

Mark then built on his visioning skills (with his wife, Emma) and set goals for himself to achieve, which ultimately keeps the whole Life Remixed™ journey on track.

Using Mark's current Yellow/Red perspective, he looks at who's involved (inspiration) and what they are doing (vision).

From Mark's original Yellow/Blue perspective, he looked at who was involved (inspiration), why they were doing this (purpose), and then later considered what (vision) and when (goals). To begin with, the Green perspective of 'how' is of less importance to a top-colour Yellow, as belief needs to be cultivated first, with the details becoming clear later in the process. 'How' can sometimes be a doubt in action and something to be aware of; however, when used positively, it can become a great asset in the planning and development of ideas.

Paul embarked on his journey to embrace the 14 Steps to a Wealthy Mindset over three decades ago. Throughout this period, his pursuit of a structured approach in defining his vision, purpose(s), value creation, and goals became evident as he cultivated a mindset aimed at wealth—not just financial wealth. In the journey towards personal and professional fulfilment, vision, for Paul, precedes purpose(s) as it lays the groundwork for direction and intentionality. Vision serves as the overarching guide, providing a panoramic view of the desired destination or outcome. It encapsulates one's long-term aspirations, ideals, and dreams, acting as a beacon that illuminates the path forward. It was the WHAT (vision), HOW (purposes), WHY (value-adding goals) of a Red/Green - Thinking/Doer. The WHO (those involved) was primarily Paul's responsibility, due to his independent personality traits.

Before pursuing specific value-adding purposes and goals, Paul articulated his vision, clarifying what he ultimately aimed to achieve. This vision served as the driving force, inspiring and motivating action towards its realisation. While value-adding purposes and goals are the specific objectives that contribute to the fulfilment of the vision, they are informed and guided by the broader vision. Each value-adding purpose and goal aligns with the overarching vision, serving as strategic waypoints along the journey towards its attainment.

The vision that Paul follows is "that of a wealthy mindset," using the 14 Steps as his guide.

Paul remarked that by establishing a clear vision first, you gain clarity and focus, enabling you to prioritise and align your purposes and value-adding goals accordingly. Vision provides a sense of purpose and meaning, infusing each endeavour with deeper significance and connection to your vision. Vision serves as the foundation upon which purposes are built, providing direction, inspiration, and coherence to one's actions and pursuits—value-adding goals. It is the starting point that ignites the journey towards realising one's fullest potential and aspirations.

This thought process allowed Paul to remain focused, follow a wealthy mindset, and achieve a place within the top 0.15% of financially wealthy individuals within the UK.

Ultimately, both authors agree and want you to realise that you are not on this planet to live someone else's dream. If you listen to everyone else and what they think you should achieve, you may well miss out on what you would love to do or could achieve. If you're not clear on your purpose(s) and vision, then everything else can be off course. When you have decided on the right vision and live 'on purpose,' you'll easily move towards your greatest achievements. We live in an ocean of motion, and nothing ever truly rests, so what will you do with your time on this planet? You wouldn't set sail without a rudder or a compass, would you? So, set your compass and align your rudder with your destination—begin with the end in mind.

When your vision and purposes are clear to you, you will decide how best to spend your time, and your value-adding goals will become clearer and more achievable.

‿

14 STEPS TO A WEALTHY MINDSET

STEP 1 - VISION

"The only thing worse than being blind is having sight but no vision,"

– Helen Keller

"If you can dream it, you can do it."

– Walt Disney, animator, film producer and entrepreneur

The different personality styles initially focus on what they deem important. Both approaches will lead you to your destination, albeit via different routes.

So, discover your E-Colours and determine what works best for you when defining your Vision and Purpose(s). The key point is that both are clearly articulated and make sense to you.

What Is a Vision?

A vision is a clear and inspiring mental image that you hold in your mind—a desired future state or outcome. It is a guiding concept that encapsulates what you aspire to achieve or become. A vision provides direction, purpose, and motivation, shaping your goals, actions, and decisions. It reflects your deepest desires, values, and aspirations, offering clarity and focus as you navigate your journey. A vision often transcends present circumstances, inspiring and mobilising individuals or organisations towards positive change and growth. It serves as a powerful beacon, guiding you towards your desired destination and guiding you through the challenges and opportunities that arise along the way. We think in pictures, and what we envision tends to come to pass—our environment is a reflection of our inner world. Visualise your perfect life, and with purpose and goals driving you, you will move towards your vision.

A simple analogy:

- My vision is to move north.
- My purpose is to walk along a road heading north.
- My goal is to walk 20 miles per day.

Knowing Where You Are Going

Having a clear vision is crucial when embarking on any journey, whether personal or professional. Without a clear destination, you'll likely find yourself wandering aimlessly, unsure of which direction to take. It's like driving in the dark without a map, no GPS, and no signposts, hoping to stumble upon your destination by chance. You deserve better than that, and you have the power to create a vision in your remarkable mind, so you must use it. Everything you currently have in your physical/material life was once a vision. Once we grasp that we have the power to create (and it's often easier to understand this by reflecting on the past), we can intentionally create moving forward. Nothing then happens by luck or coincidence. Once we take responsibility in this way, we are free to create what we genuinely desire—and we must, for life isn't a dress rehearsal. We must also ensure we pursue our desires without ever harming another person.

A Guiding Star

When you have a vision, it serves as your guiding star, affirming your sense of purpose and direction. It helps you set and achieve goals, make decisions, and stay focused on what truly matters. With a clear vision in mind, you can create a roadmap, develop strategies, and take steps that align with your desired outcome.

Life Without a Vision

Without a vision, life's journey can be frustrating and exhausting. You may encounter numerous obstacles, lose motivation, and struggle to find meaning in your actions. It's like driving in circles—wasting time, energy, and resources without making any progress. Lacking purpose and vision is a sure path to burnout as Mark experienced.

A Well-Defined Vision

On the other hand, with a well-defined and carefully crafted vision, you can make conscious choices, prioritise your efforts, and adapt to challenges along the way. Your vision acts as a beacon, guiding you towards your destination, helping you overcome obstacles, and providing a sense of fulfilment when you reach your goals.

Take Time to Pause and Reflect

At the beginning of any significant journey, it is essential to pause and reflect, seeking clarity amidst the vast expanse of choices and possibilities in today's world. Before taking that first step, it is crucial to define your vision, to know where you want the path to lead you. This moment of introspection invites you to delve deep within, to discover the core of your aspirations.

Unveiling Your True Desires

Ask yourself, with unwavering honesty, what it is that you truly desire to achieve. Allow your dreams to soar and envision the heights you wish to reach. Do not hold back here! Dare to dream. Understand that your vision is not merely a destination; it is a clear picture that will guide you through the twists, turns, and challenges ahead.

Is Your Vision a Place or a Journey?

In the realm of dreams and aspirations, the vision we hold can take on diverse forms. For some, it may manifest as a specific place, a destination to set foot upon. For others, it may be an unfolding journey, a path to traverse and explore. Regardless of its form, what truly matters is that you define this vision and embrace it with unwavering commitment. You cannot be merely interested at this point; in order to succeed, commitment to your vision is everything. There is a significant difference between being interested and being committed—which are you?

Connecting With Your Vision

In life's labyrinthine passages, it is not uncommon to feel momentarily adrift, uncertain of the road ahead. In such moments of doubt, cast your gaze once more upon your vision. Reconnect with its essence, for it is the North Star that shall guide you through the darkest of nights. Ask yourself if this vision still aligns with your deepest desires, if it still stirs passion within your soul. If so, continue down that road; if not, create a new vision and begin again. There is no such thing as failure in life—only the meaning we assign to learning events—so most of all, learn to enjoy every moment of this journey.

The Power of Dreams

Remember Walt Disney's words about the extraordinary power of dreams. Your vision, your dream, reflects your innermost emotions and desires, and it deserves to be nurtured with ardour and devotion. Mark often coaches others on releasing negative emotional attachments in their lives. Accentuating positive emotions to uplift our dreams is a hugely powerful process. When it feels good, we will do more good things, and by the laws of attraction, we attract more of the same from others. So, allow yourself the freedom to re-evaluate and redefine your vision if necessary, for it is always your right and privilege to shape your destiny. Find people who are inspired by you and support your dream, as you'll then gain real momentum.

Believing Is Seeing

In the realm of conventional wisdom, the old adage "seeing is believing" holds sway for many, and it has its uses for people at the right time and when used in a positive way. However, that saying can also be a huge limiter when used negatively. As you embark on this transformative journey, be prepared to embrace a paradigm shift, where the power of believing first becomes the catalyst for manifesting your vision. You must choose to believe something before it can ever show up in your life. Everything that has occurred in your life up to this point has happened because of the beliefs you've held until now. Taking responsibility for this fact, whether you perceive your results to be 'good' or 'bad,' is vitally important at this point in the process. So, as we move forward into your success, we welcome you to the realm of "believing is seeing."

The Power of a Vision

As an example of a well-created vision, Coca-Cola's vision is to ensure that everyone in the world has the opportunity to experience the taste of Coca-Cola. It embodies their desire to reach and connect with people from all walks of life, across borders and cultures, and offer them the unique Coca-Cola taste and experience. This vision emphasises inclusivity and the ambition to make Coca-Cola a universally recognised and enjoyed brand. By aspiring to have everyone taste Coca-Cola, the company aims to create a sense of shared enjoyment and connection, fostering moments of happiness and togetherness for individuals worldwide. There are not many people who haven't tasted Coca-Cola in the world. Could you think and create a vision of something similar to your product or services? We can. And if we can, so can you.

Google's vision is: "To organise the world's information and make it universally accessible and useful." Google's vision centres around organising and making information globally accessible, empowering individuals with knowledge, and facilitating connections across diverse fields. How many times a day do you hear the expression "Google it"?

Similarly, Microsoft's vision, "Empower every person and every organisation on the planet to achieve more," focuses on providing tools, technologies, and solutions that empower individuals, businesses, and communities to reach their full potential and accomplish their goals. There are only a few people around the world who are not aware of Microsoft's tools, technology, or solutions.

So again, start thinking about your vision—what would you like to create? Do not limit yourself here; dream big, envision big. You may hear a pessimist say not to do this because you might end up disappointed. What an incredibly limiting belief and disheartening way to live your life! We say aim for the moon, and if you miss, you'll hit a star instead. We mean for you to understand the importance of aiming high and not being afraid to 'fail' (learn). Setting a purpose, creating a vision, and then putting your ambitious goals out into the world will inspire you to work harder and push yourself further than you might otherwise.

Our Visions

For Mark and Paul, the crystallisation of Vision came with remarkable clarity. They both yearned for a journey and sought perpetual growth and purposeful fulfilment throughout that journey. Over time, both of their visions became anchored in cultivating a Wealthy Mindset—a mindset that would pave the way for abundance in all aspects of life. In the tapestry of both of their journeys, every decision they have made finds its anchor in their Visions, and the cultivation and unwavering commitment to a Wealthy Mindset. This Vision serves as the road, guiding our choices, and shaping the trajectory of their lives—it is truly their Vision.

The First Step – Creating Your Vision

In the realms of self-awareness, self-discovery, and self-development, we implore you to revisit the fundamental question once more: What is it that you truly desire to achieve? With renewed curiosity, ask yourself better questions, and you'll always get better answers. And while you do this, let your dreams soar freely, unencumbered by constraints. DO NOT ALLOW NEGATIVITY IN HERE, from your own mind or from the minds of others. Envision the heights you yearn to reach with your vision, painting a vivid picture on the canvas of your mind. Create a vision board for you to look at daily, and cover it with pictures of things you'd like to experience. Mark created a 'multiple sources of income' map and looks at it often—remember, believing is seeing. Things will show up in your life once you believe. Multiple revenue streams are an important part of building financial wealth.

Your vision does not need to match that of Coca-Cola, Microsoft, or Google; however, it does need to be something that you can relate to, embrace, and follow with passion—it's your vision. It does not have to be unique; you can and will be inspired by others. However, make your vision your own. Create your own vision board today, and start to create your perfect life on it. Add photos and inspiring messages to yourself. Do not listen to your mind if it is telling you 'This is stupid, it will never happen.' As Henry Ford said, "Whether you think you can or think you can't, you're right." So, get creative, dream big, think realistically and break it down, feel good about it, and get it done. You'll be amazed at how quickly you will start to attract these visions into your life.

CHAPTER 6

14 STEPS TO A WEALTHY MINDSET

STEP 2 - PURPOSE(S)

"Your purpose in life is to find your purpose and give your whole heart and soul to it."

– Buddha

Do you have a definite purpose or purposes that guide your ambitions and vision?

Napoleon Hill wrote, "What a different story people would have to tell if they would adopt a definite purpose and stand by that purpose until it had time to become an all-consuming purpose."

If you fail to define your purpose, everything else falls out of alignment. It's like using a broken compass—you may think you're heading in the right direction, but you're not. Most of the time, you're unsure which way you're going, so you end up wandering aimlessly, never fully feeling in the flow of things.

It is crucial to discover what you're good at, what you love doing, and then do it. It's remarkable how often people know what they love but believe they can't make money from it. Remember Henry Ford's words: "Whether you think you can or think you can't, you're right." Don't waste time thinking about why you can't do something—you can earn money doing almost anything. Multiple sources of income are key here.

However, a note of caution: be sensible about what you aim to achieve. We know many people who love playing the piano, but that doesn't mean they're skilled enough to make it a full-time career. Sometimes, you must balance doing what you're good at with what you're passionate about to make money.

Psychologist Alfred Adler once said, "I am grateful for the idea that has used me." When you fall in love with an idea, it guides you—you don't guide it anymore.

Purpose gives meaning to WHY you're doing what you're doing.

Mark's clearly defined life purpose, which came to him well after the age of 40, is "to bring joy and knowledge, to inspire and create, so that other people learn to live, love, and enjoy their lives to the full." By living this way, Mark has decided to live "on purpose," meaning there are no accidents—luck and coincidence don't factor in. This clear definition of purpose has allowed Mark to attract more happiness, health, wealth, great relationships with friends and family, and continuous business opportunities, ensuring that his vision and all his significant goals are consistently met.

Everything must connect back to your purpose in life, especially when it comes to building and protecting financial wealth. As we grow, layers of purpose can be outgrown and shed, so always believe you can follow a different path. Paul has identified eight purposes in his life and continues to seek ways to not only maintain but grow his position within the top 0.15% of net-worth individuals within the UK as part of these purposes.

What Is Your Purpose in Life?

Determining your purpose(s) in life is a deeply personal and introspective journey. It can vary greatly from person to person, influenced by individual values, passions, beliefs, and experiences. Here are some common purposes people often strive for:

Self-Realisation: Many seek personal growth, self-discovery, and fulfilment as their primary purpose in life. This involves understanding oneself, exploring talents and interests, and striving to reach one's full potential.

Making a Positive Impact: Some find purpose in making a difference in the lives of others or in the world at large. They may pursue careers or activities that contribute to social, environmental, or humanitarian causes.

Building Meaningful Relationships: For many, life's purpose revolves around cultivating and nurturing deep connections with family, friends, and loved ones. They prioritise relationships and strive to create a supportive and loving network.

Pursuing Passions and Talents: Some find purpose in pursuing their passions, hobbies, or talents. They engage in activities that bring them joy, satisfaction, and a sense of accomplishment, whether it's art, music, sports, coaching, or any other creative outlet.

Seeking Knowledge and Wisdom: The pursuit of knowledge, learning, and personal growth can be a significant purpose in life. This may involve continuous education, intellectual exploration, and seeking wisdom through reading, travel, or philosophical discussions.

Spiritual or Religious Quest: Many find purpose through spirituality or religion. They seek a deeper understanding of their beliefs, a connection to a higher power, and a sense of meaning and purpose guided by their faith.

Personal Well-being and Happiness: For some, life's purpose is simply to prioritise their well-being and happiness. They strive to live a fulfilling and balanced life, taking care of their physical, emotional, and mental health.

Building Financial Wealth: Many believe that by building wealth, they can empower themselves and those around them, opening doors to a brighter future and paving the way for others to thrive. With each passing day, as they delve deeper into the intricacies of finance, they feel a growing sense of purpose, knowing that their journey is not just about accumulating wealth but about transforming lives and forging a path towards a life of abundance and possibility.

It's important to note that these purposes are not mutually exclusive, and an individual may find fulfilment in a combination of them or have different purposes at different stages of life. Ultimately, finding purpose is a personal journey that requires self-reflection, exploration, and aligning one's actions with their values and aspirations.

Having a sense of purpose can provide numerous benefits, including increased resilience, motivation, and overall well-being. It gives us a reason to get out of bed in the morning, fuels our drive to overcome challenges, and brings a sense of fulfilment and satisfaction.

Writing down your purpose in life can be a powerful and beneficial practice for several reasons:

Clarity, Vision, and Focus: Writing down your purpose helps you gain clarity about what truly matters to you. It forces you to reflect on your vision, values, and aspirations, helping you articulate them in a tangible form. By doing so, you create a clear roadmap for your life, guiding your decisions and actions.

Goal Setting: When you write down your purpose, you can convert it into specific, actionable goals. By setting clear objectives, you create a sense of direction and motivation. Goals help you stay focused and provide a benchmark for measuring your progress. You can start small and grow—now we set 90-day goals and then move to 1, 3, 5, and 10-year goals.

Commitment and Accountability: Putting your purpose in writing signifies a commitment to yourself. It serves as a reminder of your intentions and helps you stay accountable to your purpose. With a written record, you can refer back to it regularly and evaluate whether your actions align with your purpose.

Overcoming Obstacles: Life often presents challenges and obstacles that may deter you from pursuing your purpose.

However, a written statement of your purpose can serve as a source of inspiration and motivation during difficult times. It can remind you of your overarching vision and help you stay resilient.

Personal Growth and Alignment: Writing down your purpose can be a reflective exercise that deepens your self-awareness. It encourages you to contemplate your strengths, passions, and values, enabling you to align your life choices with what truly matters. This alignment fosters personal growth, fulfilment, and a sense of meaning.

Communication and Collaboration: Sharing your written purpose with others can foster deeper connections and collaboration. When you clearly express your purpose, you invite like-minded individuals into your life who can support and collaborate with you on your journey.

Work Smarter, Not Harder: Balance your life by prioritising your time. These priorities should be based on your purpose(s) in life. Many people think that we must work hard for money, yet some of the wealthiest people are seldom seen working—how can that be? Defining purpose(s) will help you work smarter, create better ideas that inspire others, and ultimately help you prevent burnout. It will make you feel good and move you quickly towards your vision. One of the greatest advantages we see is working hard to show our worth, so don't confuse working smarter with a lazy attitude—it's quite the opposite.

Remember that your purpose(s) in life may evolve over time as you gain new experiences and insights. Revisiting and updating your written purpose(s) periodically can help ensure they remain relevant and aligned with your current aspirations.

Overall, writing down your purpose(s) in life can be a powerful tool for self-reflection, goal setting, commitment, and personal growth. It serves as a constant reminder of what you strive to achieve and can significantly influence your actions and decisions, ultimately leading to a more fulfilling and purpose-driven life.

How Did We Find Our Own Purpose(s) in Life?

Finding our own purpose in life was a personal and introspective journey that required self-reflection, exploration, and self-discovery. It involved understanding our values, interests, strengths, and passions. We reflected on what brings us joy, what activities make us feel energised and fulfilled, and considered the impact we would like to make in the world.

In the depths of self-reflection, Paul's journey of exploration and self-discovery unfolded, leading him to crystallise eight profound purposes and ideas into his life. Each purpose holds a significance that resonates within himself, shaping his aspirations and igniting a fire that drives him onward:

1. **Providing for his family now**: Nurturing and providing for his family in the present moment, ensuring their well-being and happiness. If we consider his priorities in the following order as needs/investing/wants, providing for his family now is all about their needs in life. Without providing for these needs, such as food, shelter, clothing, healthcare, and education, then their ability to survive and prosper is somewhat limited.

2. **Financial independence**: Striving for financial independence, a state where the fruits of his labours flourish, allowing him to live without reliance on external income or government support. Being able to create his own financial independence and that of his family is important to him. So is helping those around him with financial knowledge.

3. **Continually growing financial wealth**: Embarking on an unwavering pursuit to expand and grow financial wealth, continually seeking opportunities to maximise potential and abundance. Maintaining and growing his financial wealth within the top 0.15% (within the UK). Assisting those around him in growing their financial wealth. It is this purpose along with purpose #2 that will allow purposes #1, #4, #5 & #6 to flourish.

4. **Freedom with how he uses his time**: Aiming for a level of freedom that transcends conventional limitations, granting him autonomy over how he utilises his time, fostering a life of intentional choices. These choices will allow him to prioritise how he allocates his time and how he can help those around him who need it.

5. **Spending time with his family**: Cherishing the precious moments spent with family, creating memories that transcend time and bring them closer together.

6. **Controlled, guilt-free spending**: Embracing the joy of indulging in select luxuries with a mindful approach, savouring guilt-free spending that elevates the lives of our loved ones and himself—whether it's a token of appreciation for his wife and son or fulfilling dreams like business and first-class travel and comfortable

homes. These are some of his wants that once you have reached financial independence you can afford to have too. That does not mean you forget about the needs/ investing priorities.

7. **Securing a wealthy future for his family**: Cultivating a wealthy mindset for his family, diligently securing a prosperous future for his loved ones, encompassing financial abundance and abundance of the heart.

8. **Legacy**: Committing to unwavering integrity and doing the right thing, recognising that every action or inaction shapes the legacy that he will leave behind—a legacy built upon moral virtue and positive impact.

These eight ideas, crafted through deep introspection, are not stagnant but living entities that demand constant evaluation. To truly embody them, Paul must weave them into the very fabric of his existence, continuously assessing their relevance and aligning his actions with their profound essence. Through this dedication and conscious choice, Paul strives to lead a life of purpose, meaning, and boundless contribution, enriching not only his journey but the lives of those around him.

Our chosen purpose(s) in life keep us on track, and what you focus your energy on gets done. Where attention goes, energy flows.

Finding Your Purpose(s) in Life

Finding your purpose(s) in life is a personal and introspective journey that requires self-reflection, exploration, and self-discovery, as mentioned previously. It involves understanding your values, interests, strengths, and passions. It also involves having a vision aligned with your purpose(s). Reflect on what brings you joy, what activities make you feel energised and fulfilled, and consider the impact you want to make in the world. It can be helpful to ask yourself meaningful questions, such as:

- What is my vision?
- What are my ethics and beliefs?
- What am I passionate about in life?
- What am I good at in life?
- What did I enjoy before I was 10 years old?
- What activities or causes am I naturally drawn to?
- What are my unique talents, skills, and strengths?
- What are my potential limiters?
- What issues or problems in the world resonate with me that I can help solve?
- Do I make enough money?
- Would I like to make more money?
- What do I want to be remembered for?
- What would my perfect day look like?
- What would my perfect week look like?
- What would my perfect year look like?
- What do I really want from my life?

It's important to remember that your purpose(s) could evolve over time as you grow, learn, and gain new perspectives. Your purpose(s) needs to be continually reviewed and adjusted if needed. Don't be afraid to change your purpose(s) in life—but change for the right reasons, not just for the sake of change.

Once you find your purpose(s) in life, decide to give your whole heart and soul towards achieving it.

Your purpose(s) will guide you and help you decide how to spend your time. Clearly defined purpose(s) will also help you prevent burnout and navigate any challenges. Your life will be wonderful as a result of living 'on purpose'.

CHAPTER 6

⌒

14 STEPS TO A WEALTHY MINDSET

STEP 3 - CREATING VALUE

"Try not to become a man of success, but a man of value."

– Albert Einstein

What Is Money?

Money is energy. Yes, you read that correctly. Money is pure energy, and to attract it into our lives and enjoy it, we must cultivate an abundance of personal energy and hold the right attitude about money itself.

Let's examine a few common money beliefs:

- Money doesn't grow on trees.
- Who do you think I am? Branson? Rockefeller?
- I'm not made of money!
- We don't have enough money.

- We can't afford it.
- Money is evil.
- Money doesn't buy happiness.
- People will hate you if you're rich.
- More money means more problems.
- The pursuit of money is bad.

These are many people's core beliefs, and they can have a particularly negative impact on financial health: money avoidance, money worship, and money status are just a few. Such beliefs are linked to lower net worth, lower income, and higher levels of debt.

Money is simply a tool, a medium of exchange that helps us acquire what we desire—whether it's financial independence, time to spend with family, a bigger house, a car, a plane, or even a club.

Those who achieve greatness don't let limiting money beliefs and negative thoughts control them.

Money magnifies who we already are.

So, money will make you more of what you already are. Take a few minutes, and reflect on that for a moment.

What kind of person would you be if you had more money right now? Would you be someone amazing who helps others grow?

Mark loves this phrase: Love People – Use Money. Many people mistakenly reverse this, and it can truly destroy their happiness.

Paul, however, notes that this can also be a reflection of personality styles. People-oriented personalities (Yellow & Blue) prioritise people first, while task-oriented personalities (Red & Green) focus on money generation as the primary task.

From Paul's perspective, "Generate Money – Love People" is the complementary opposite side of the coin. Both perspectives are valid; they're just different ways of viewing things.

While some wealthy people may use their money for selfish reasons, that's not the case for everyone, nor is it the true meaning of financial wealth. Sweeping generalisations and negative beliefs about wealth can be destructive.

If Mark had received millions of pounds as a younger man, it would likely have destroyed him. Nowadays, he is very comfortable with the idea of great wealth and using money as a tool for doing good.

Mark has met incredibly wealthy people who turned out to be some of the most genuine and generous individuals he's had the pleasure of knowing.

As we've said, different people have different mindsets.

Money is neither good nor evil; it becomes what the person holding it makes of it.

This is where self-development becomes crucial. The more Mark has developed himself, the more money he has earned, and this continues to be true. The same will apply to you. Go back and read or listen to *Life Remixed* to truly develop yourself and raise your income. Start today.

Once you have true love and acceptance for people in your heart, you can start enjoying life and making more money.

Mark has asked thousands of coaching clients over the years: how do you earn money? Most reply, 'I have a job, and I go to work,' which is the answer society has taught us.

The answer we're looking for is, 'I give great service to humanity,' and 'I create value wherever I go and at every opportunity.'

Paul's advice is to choose a vocation you're good at—focus on creating value, aligned with your passion (if you're good at it), and you'll enjoy every moment of your life.

What Is Value?

Value refers to the worth or importance assigned to something. It can be subjective and varies from person to person or context to context. Value can be measured in various ways, such as in monetary terms, utility, or personal significance.

In economics, value often refers to the monetary worth of goods or services. The value of an item is determined by factors like supply and demand, scarcity, production costs, and the utility it provides to individuals or society.

In ethics and philosophy, value can refer to moral or ethical principles and the worthiness of certain actions or behaviours. Different ethical theories propose various sources of value, such as maximising happiness (utilitarianism), respecting individual rights (deontology), or adhering to virtues (virtue ethics).

Value can also be subjective and personal, relating to individual preferences, beliefs, and priorities. People assign value to things based on their own desires, needs, and goals. For example, someone may value experiences, relationships, personal growth, or certain possessions.

It's important to remember that value is a multifaceted concept, and its interpretation can differ depending on the context in which it's used.

When considering value creation from a wealthy mindset perspective, you must account for all these multifaceted definitions: monetary terms, ethics and philosophy, and personal significance.

How Do You Create Value?

Creating value typically involves generating or enhancing something that is considered beneficial or desirable to others. Here are some ways to create value:

Meeting needs and solving problems: Identify the needs, challenges, or pain points of your target audience and develop products, services, or solutions that address those issues effectively.

Innovation and improvement: Introduce new ideas, technologies, or processes that enhance existing products or services, making them more efficient, convenient, or enjoyable.

Quality and reliability: Focus on delivering high-quality products or services that consistently meet or exceed customer expectations. Reliability and consistency help build trust and loyalty.

Customisation and personalisation: Tailor offerings to individual customer preferences, providing personalised experiences, recommendations, or solutions.

Efficiency and cost-effectiveness: Streamline processes, optimise resources, and find ways to reduce costs without compromising quality, passing the savings on to customers.

Convenience and accessibility: Simplify the customer experience, make products or services easily accessible, and remove barriers to entry or usage.

Enhancing experiences: Consider the overall customer journey, and find ways to improve it through exceptional service, unique features, or memorable interactions.

Social and environmental responsibility: Incorporate sustainable practices, ethical standards, and social responsibility into business operations, demonstrating a commitment to the greater good.

Collaboration and partnerships: Seek opportunities to collaborate with other businesses or individuals to combine strengths, resources, and expertise, creating synergies and added value.

Continuous learning and adaptation: Stay agile and adaptable, continuously learning from customer feedback, market trends, and industry developments to innovate and improve offerings over time.

It's essential to understand the specific needs and desires of your target audience and be able to adapt based on changing circumstances and feedback.

How Do You Monetise Value?

Monetising value refers to converting the value you've created into financial returns or revenue. Here are common strategies for monetising value:

Direct sales: Offer products or services to customers and generate revenue through sales transactions. This can include selling physical goods, digital products, software licences, or access to services.

Subscription model: Provide ongoing value through a subscription-based model, where customers pay a recurring fee for access to products, services, or exclusive content.

Freemium model: Offer a basic version or limited access to your product or service for free while providing additional features or premium content at a cost. This allows customers to experience the value before deciding to upgrade or purchase add-ons.

Licensing or royalties: If you've created intellectual property, such as patents, copyrights, or trademarks, you can licence the rights to others in exchange for licensing fees or royalties based on usage or sales.

Advertising and sponsorship: If your platform or content attracts a large audience, you can monetise it through advertising by displaying ads or partnering with brands for sponsored content or endorsements.

Affiliate marketing: Promote products or services of other companies, and earn a commission for every sale or referral generated through your marketing efforts. This can be done through affiliate links, coupon codes, or dedicated referral programmes.

Data monetisation: If you collect valuable data from your users or customers, you can anonymise and aggregate it to provide insights or sell it to other businesses or researchers who can benefit from the information.

Consulting or services: Leverage your expertise or the value you've created to offer consulting services, training programmes, workshops, or customised solutions for clients who are willing to pay for your specialised knowledge.

Licensing or franchising: If you've developed a successful business model, brand, or concept, you can licence or franchise it to others, allowing them to operate their own businesses using your established framework in exchange for fees or royalties.

Partnerships and collaborations: Form strategic partnerships or collaborations with other businesses to jointly create and monetise value. This can involve revenue sharing, cross-promotion, or co-development of products or services.

It's important to consider your value proposition, target market, and industry when selecting the most suitable monetisation strategy. Experimentation, market research, and understanding your customers' willingness to pay are crucial in determining the most effective approach to monetising value. Knowing your market is key to achieving the right monetised value.

Over the past three decades, we've found that exceeding expectations in both relationships and work is a great strategy for gaining an advantage and creating additional leverage—do that little bit more, and it will always come back to you later.

How Did We Approach Value Creation for This Book?

For many authors, writing and sharing thoughts, ideas, and stories align with their personal and creative fulfilment. In this book, we aimed to create value for you, the reader, by sharing the Steps of a Wealthy Mindset. Here's how we created value in this book:

Expressing creativity: We've tapped into our creative abilities to produce unique and imaginative works that entertain, inspire, or provoke thought.

Sharing knowledge and insights: We've shared our expertise, knowledge, and insights on wealth mindset and financial success. This can help others gain new perspectives, learn, and grow in various areas of interest.

Provoking thought and challenging perspectives: We've presented thought-provoking ideas or themes, encouraging readers to question conventional thinking, expand their worldview, and initiate meaningful conversations.

Inspiring and motivating others: By sharing personal experiences, overcoming challenges, and offering advice, we hope to inspire readers to pursue their dreams, achieve personal growth, or overcome obstacles in their lives.

Educating and raising awareness: We've written about important issues, shedding light on topics that require attention, and sparking conversations or actions for positive change.

The value created by an author is subjective and varies depending on the reader's perspective and individual preferences.

However, aligning writing with one's purpose and passion often leads to a more fulfilling and meaningful creative journey.

How Did We View Value Creation for Paul's Purpose(s) in Life?

Creating value for Paul's purpose(s) in life involves deliberate actions and choices that align with his purpose(s) and ethics. This value creation can benefit both Paul and others. Here are some of the values that worked for Paul:

Providing for his Family Now:

- Ensure a stable income by pursuing opportunities that align with Paul's skills and interests.
- Prioritise the well-being of Paul's family by meeting their basic needs, such as food, shelter, and healthcare.
- Allocate time and resources for activities that bring joy and create meaningful experiences with Paul's family.

Spending Time with his Family:

- Make a conscious effort to prioritise family time in his schedule.
- Plan and engage in activities that foster connection and create lasting memories.
- Actively listen and engage in meaningful conversations to strengthen their bonds.

Securing a Wealthy Future for his Family:

- Educate his family about a wealthy mindset. This book will act as a great reference guide.

Freedom with How He Uses His Time:

- Evaluate his commitments and obligations, ensuring they align with his priorities and goals.

- Practice effective time management techniques to optimise his productivity and create space for activities that bring him joy and fulfilment.

- Set boundaries and learn to say "no" to tasks or responsibilities that do not align with his goals.

Financial Independence:

- Focus on building assets and reducing debt to achieve financial independence.

- Know the difference between assets and liabilities, in both people and finances.

- Develop a comprehensive financial plan that encompasses priorities, savings, expenses, and long-term investments.

- Keep his financial plan current.

- Continuously seek opportunities to enhance his financial knowledge and skills.

- Spend less than him earn, saving 10%, 20%, 50%, or even 75% of his earnings steadily, depending on his situation, allowing him to sleep well at night.

Continually Growing his Financial Wealth:

- Set targets for his financial growth.
- Monitor his financial progress regularly.

- Stay informed about financial trends, investment opportunities, and strategies for wealth accumulation and circulation.
- Seek professional advice from financial advisors or experts to make informed investment decisions.
- Embrace a wealthy mindset, surround yourself with like-minded individuals, and consistently seek personal and professional development opportunities to maximise his earning potential, while always sharing with others.

Controlled Guilt-Free Spending:

- Create priorities that allow for guilt-free spending on items or experiences that align with his wealthy mindset and bring happiness to his family.
- Prioritise and allocate funds for meaningful experiences or items that provide long-term satisfaction rather than short-lived gratification.
- Practice mindful spending by considering the impact and value of each purchase before deciding.

Legacy:

- Lead by example, and make decisions based on his wealthy mindset. Start with ethics as a foundation, followed by the other components of his mindset.
- Engage in philanthropic activities or support causes that align with his values and create a positive impact on society.
- Share his knowledge and experiences with his family and community to inspire and empower others.

Remember, creating value for your purpose(s) in life is a continuous journey. It requires self-reflection, intentional decision-making, and a commitment to aligning your actions with your goals and ethics. It's about creating value for yourself and others. When we discuss goals in the next chapter, these must stem from the values you have created alongside your vision and purpose(s) in life.

CHAPTER 6

~~~~~

14 STEPS TO A WEALTHY MINDSET

STEP 4 - GOALS

"Setting goals is the first step in turning the invisible into the visible."

– Tony Robbins, motivational speaker

The best thing about setting a goal is who you become in the process of achieving it. That's why we encourage people in Life Remixed™ coaching to set big goals, even if they have no idea how to achieve them. When they do achieve those goals, they realise two things: that they can accomplish what they set their minds to, and they have grown as individuals in the process. Then, they're ready to set new goals and continue the growth journey.

The number one aspect of setting goals is that we must "grow." If we don't grow, we won't be fulfilled. Every healthy human being is committed to some kind of growth in an area of their life. The second is that we must contribute beyond ourselves.

If our goals only serve our own pleasure, achieving them will bring only short-lived happiness. When your mission is to serve others, you not only leave a legacy of giving but you also find greater fulfilment in life. Essentially, your path to fulfilment is paved with growth and giving.

For these reasons, setting goals is a crucial step in transforming your purpose into a tangible reality. Goals provide direction, motivation, and a clear path towards achieving what you want in life. By setting specific, measurable, achievable, relevant, and time-bound (SMART) GOALS, you create a framework that guides your actions and helps you stay focused as you move towards your huge, seemingly unattainable goals.

Here's how setting goals can help you turn your purpose in life into reality:

Clarity and Focus: Goals help you gain clarity about what you truly desire. They provide a specific target and help you focus your efforts and energy in the right direction.

Motivation and Inspiration: Well-defined goals ignite your motivation and give you a sense of purpose. Goals create a vision of what you want to accomplish, inspiring you to take consistent action to achieve them.

Action Planning: Setting goals involves breaking down your purpose and value creation into smaller, actionable steps. By outlining the necessary actions and milestones, you create a roadmap that brings you closer to your purpose.

Progress Tracking: Goals allow you to measure your progress. By monitoring your achievements against your goals, you can identify what's working and make adjustments if needed. This tracking process keeps you on track and helps maintain momentum.

Overcoming Obstacles: Goals provide a framework for overcoming challenges along the way. When faced with setbacks, you can reassess your approach, find alternative solutions, and adjust your goals if necessary. This flexibility allows you to adapt while still pursuing your purpose.

Accountability and Discipline: Setting goals creates a sense of accountability. You become responsible for your progress and results. This accountability fosters discipline and helps you stay committed, even when faced with distractions or setbacks.

Personal Growth and Development: Pursuing meaningful goals pushes you out of your comfort zone and encourages personal growth. It challenges you to acquire new skills, expand your knowledge, and develop qualities that contribute to your success.

Remember, goal setting is not a one-time activity. It's a continuous process that evolves as you grow and progress, gaining new insights on your journey. Regularly setting, reassessing, and achieving your goals, and adjusting them as needed, ensures that you stay aligned with your purpose and vision. By understanding that you are the creator of your reality and that you create with your thoughts and feelings, you can keep moving forward with a clearly defined purpose, vision, and goals, ultimately turning them into reality.

How Do You Set SMART GOALS?

GOALS are such an important part of a wealthy mindset that from hereon in, these will be shown as "GOALS" so we highlight this importance.

Setting GOALS for achieving your purpose in life involves a deliberate and thoughtful process that includes how you will create value. Here's a step-by-step guide to help you set effective GOALS:

1. **Reflect on Your Purpose(s)**: Take time to reflect on your purpose(s) in life. What do you value most? What brings you joy and fulfilment? Understanding your purpose(s) provides a strong foundation for setting meaningful GOALS aligned with what you are good at or your passion and value creation.

2. **Define Specific GOALS**: Once you have a clear understanding of your purpose(s), translate it into specific GOALS by looking at how you create value. A specific GOAL is well-defined and clearly states what you want to achieve. For example, if your purpose(s) is to make a positive impact on the environment, a specific GOAL could be to start a recycling initiative in your community.

3. **Make GOALS Measurable**: Set measurable GOALS that allow you to track your progress and determine when you've achieved them. Measurable GOALS have tangible criteria for success. For instance, if your GOAL is to improve your physical fitness, you could set a measurable GOAL of running a 10K race within a specific timeframe.

4. **Ensure GOALS Are Achievable**: Your 90-day to 1-year GOALS should be challenging yet attainable. Assess your resources, abilities, and current circumstances to determine if your GOALS are realistic. Setting overly ambitious GOALS that are beyond your reach can lead to frustration and discouragement. However, maintain belief, and set a huge GOAL to motivate yourself daily (but don't get emotionally attached to the outcome, as this could lead to disappointment).

5. **Set Relevant GOALS**: Your GOALS should be relevant and meaningful in relation to your purpose(s) in life and how they will create value. Consider how each GOAL aligns with your value creation and long-term aspirations. Ensure that pursuing these GOALS will contribute to your overall sense of fulfilment.

6. **Time-Bound GOALS**: Assign deadlines or timeframes to your GOALS. A time-bound GOAL creates a sense of urgency and helps you stay focused. It also enables you to break down your GOALS into smaller, manageable tasks and establish a timeline for achieving them. We usually start with 90-day GOALS and build from there to 1, 3, 5, and 10 year goals.

7. **Create an Action Plan**: Break down your GOALS into actionable steps. Identify the specific actions, resources, and support you need to accomplish each GOAL. Create a detailed action plan that outlines the necessary tasks, milestones, and deadlines.

8. **Track Progress and Adjust**: Regularly monitor your progress towards your GOALS. Celebrate your achievements and adjust if needed. Assess whether your

GOALS are still aligned with your purpose and value creation, and make revisions as necessary to ensure continued growth and alignment.

9. **Stay Accountable**: Share your GOALS with trusted individuals who can support and hold you accountable. Consider finding an accountability partner or joining a supportive community where you can share progress, receive feedback, and stay motivated.

Remember, setting GOALS is a dynamic process. As you grow and evolve, your GOALS may change or expand. Stay open to new possibilities and regularly reassess your GOALS to ensure they continue to reflect your vision, purpose(s), and value creation.

Examples of SMART GOALS:

You will see from the following examples how Paul has defined his purpose(s) based on what he wanted from life (Chapter 6 – Step 2 – Purpose), showed the value these GOALS would bring to his life, and then used the guidance above to establish SMART GOALS.

Purpose – Creating Value – GOALS

Providing for His Family Now:

Ensure a stable income by pursuing opportunities aligned with your skills and interests.

- GOAL: Achieve a monthly revenue of GBP or USD [insert your target number] from two companies to cover outgoing costs by utilising your skills and interests.

Prioritise the well-being of my family by meeting their basic needs, such as food, shelter, and healthcare.

- GOAL: Set a monthly budget of GBP or USD [insert your monthly amount] and track these expenses monthly.

- GOAL: Allocate time and resources for activities that bring joy and create meaningful experiences for my family.

- GOAL: Dedicate weekends to family time, limiting work activities to emergency situations only.

- GOAL: Engage in activities that make your family happy [insert what these activities are].

Spending Quality Time with the Family:

Make a conscious effort to prioritise family time in your schedule.

- GOAL: Reserve weekends exclusively for family time.

- GOAL: Plan and book the next trip to visit family by [insert the time for when this will happen, and when you will book the travel]. Include this in your schedule and daily tasks.

Plan and engage in activities that foster connection and create lasting memories.

- GOAL: Plan activities to enjoy with family during your next visit [insert what you will do].

Actively listen and engage in meaningful conversations to strengthen your bond.

- GOAL: Schedule daily FaceTime calls with family, ensuring you pause and actively listen during conversations.
- GOAL: Track these conversations and set goals for improvement opportunities [insert what you will do for improvement].

Securing a Wealthy Future for His Family:

Educate your family about a wealthy mindset. This book will serve as a valuable reference guide.

- GOAL: Dedicate 2 hours each week to educate my wife and son about a wealthy mindset using the contents of this book.
- GOAL: Use my financial wealth planner to teach my wife how to track issues such as bank access, financial worth, revenues, and expenses. Spend 2 hours each week on this.

Freedom with How You Use Your Time:

Evaluate your commitments and obligations, ensuring they align with your priorities and goals.

- GOAL: Maintain a daily list of action items.
- GOAL: Prioritise your actions each morning.
- GOAL: Use synchronised notes across devices for better organisation.

Practice effective time management techniques to optimise productivity and create space for activities that bring joy and fulfilment.

- GOAL: Avoid multitasking.

- GOAL: Stay focused on the task at hand.
- GOAL: Remove clutter and distractions by switching off alerts and choosing work locations that minimise background noise.
- GOAL: Continuously manage your time using your action items list throughout each day.

Set boundaries and learn to say "no" to tasks or responsibilities that do not align with your GOALS.

- GOAL: Use your E-Colours to avoid conflicts by saying no in a polite and considerate way—respond rather than react, hit your pause button, think about the other person's E-Colours, and respond appropriately.

Financial Independence:

Focus on building assets and eliminating debt to achieve financial independence.

- GOAL: Include in your tasks a regular check on credit cards, and ensure timely payments.
- GOAL: Track your net worth by asset class, e.g., cash, gold, silver, properties, bonds, equities, alternatives, currency, companies, whiskey, watches, etc.

Develop a comprehensive financial plan that encompasses priorities, savings, and long-term investing.

- GOAL: Review your financial planner weekly.
- GOAL: Track your future plans weekly, e.g., a new venture with a partner.

Keep your financial plan current.

- GOAL: Continue to track your financial planner weekly.
- GOAL: Monitor future ventures weekly, e.g., a new venture with a partner.

Continuously seek opportunities to enhance your financial knowledge and skills.

- GOAL: Dedicate 1 to 2 hours per day to self-development.

Continually Growing His Financial Wealth and Increasing His Position within the UK's Top 0.15% of Wealthy Individuals:

Set an annual target to grow your financial wealth.

- GOAL: Achieve a target of GBP or USD [insert your target number] within the next year.

Stay informed about financial trends, investment opportunities, and strategies for wealth accumulation.

- GOAL: Dedicate 1 to 2 hours per day to self-development.

Seek professional advice from financial advisors or experts to make informed investment decisions.

- GOAL: Receive semi-monthly updates from a wealth management company on your investment portfolio. Review and update as necessary, including exploring new opportunities, e.g., a recent investment in a biotech company.

- GOAL: Begin searching for property investment experts within the next month.

Embrace a wealthy mindset, surround yourself with like-minded individuals, and consistently seek personal and professional development opportunities to maximise your earning potential while always sharing with others.

- GOAL: Add one new person to your wealthy mindset group each month.
- GOAL: Continue with activities like the Life Remixed™ Book Club.

Controlled Guilt-Free Spending:

Create priorities that allow for guilt-free spending on items or experiences that align with his wealthy mindset and bring happiness to my family.

- GOAL: Plan 2 family trips per year, business class, booking 6 months in advance, and include these in my schedule.
- GOAL: Plan 2 personal trips per year, business class, booking 6 months in advance, and include these in my schedule.
- GOAL: Schedule 2 shopping trips with my wife, and include these in my calendar.

Prioritise and allocate funds for meaningful experiences or items that provide long-term satisfaction rather than short-lived gratification.

- GOAL: Budget for 2 family trips at GBP or USD [insert the amount per trip].

- GOAL: Budget for 2 personal trips at GBP or USD [insert the amount per trip].

- GOAL: Budget for 2 shopping trips with my wife at GBP or USD [insert the amount per trip].

Practice mindful spending by considering the impact and value of each purchase before deciding.

- GOAL: Include guilt-free spending in your expense projections, and review them each week.

Legacy:

Lead by example and make decisions based on your wealthy mindset. Begin with your ethics as the foundation of all decisions, followed by the steps of your wealthy mindset.

- GOAL: Continuously evaluate and, if necessary, adjust your ethics each month—respect, trust, integrity, honesty, gratitude, financial discipline, compassion, understanding, forgiveness, courage, goodwill, desire to succeed, and enjoyment.

Engage in philanthropic activities, or support causes that align with your values and create a positive impact on society.

- GOAL: Make annual contributions to the homeless on each of your birthdays—GBP or USD [insert your target number] per birthday. Include this in your daily priority list and schedule.

Share your knowledge and experiences with your family and community to inspire and empower others.

- GOAL: Use the contents of this book to share and inspire within your community.
- GOAL: Use the contents of this book to coach your family.
- GOAL: Respond to those who ask for help.

Start investing in yourself as early as possible. If you're struggling to find enough money to invest, consider deciding to earn more money by adding value to other people's lives or by doing things that others are not willing to do, or to spend less, perhaps by cutting out certain habits. We've known Life Remixed™ coaching clients who have saved thousands by quitting alcohol or smoking, and this money can then be redirected into creative investments that will clearly serve them far better in the long run.

On the journey to a wealthy mindset, turning your purpose(s) and vision into tangible, value-driven GOALS is crucial. It's through this process that you begin to shape your dreams and aspirations into reality.

However, merely conceptualising your purpose(s) and potential value isn't enough. To truly make a difference and achieve your desired outcomes, it's essential to translate these ideas into GOALS that are actionable steps. These GOALS serve as a roadmap, guiding your actions and decisions towards success.

But setting GOALS is just the beginning; real transformation happens when you take action. You must be willing to step out of your comfort zone, embrace challenges, and persistently work towards these GOALS. It's not enough to be merely interested in achieving; you must be fully committed, giving all your available focus and attention to your pursuits. When it gets tough, remind yourself of how incredible it will feel to create your purpose(s), vision, and GOALS, and to give the gift of joy and happiness to yourself, your loved ones, and the world.

Satisfaction

Satisfaction is defined as what you have divided by what you want. Today, Mark and Paul both stand at 100% on their satisfaction curve. They continuously monitor and adjust their vision, purpose(s), value creation, and GOALS. Their GOALS are aligned with their position on the satisfaction curve. This becomes a powerful source of motivation and inspiration—so be sure to pay attention to small wins and celebrate them daily, weekly, and monthly.

Remember, it's the combination of vision, purpose(s), value creation, and the achievement of actionable GOALS through decisive action that propels you towards meaningful outcomes and a life of daily abundance and fulfilment. Embrace this transformative journey of a wealthy mindset, and watch with joy as you become the creator of your own destiny, turning the invisible into the visible.

~~~~~~

14 STEPS TO A WEALTHY MINDSET

STEP 5 - ETHICS

"The time is always right to do what is right."

– Martin Luther King JR,
activist in American civil rights

Ethics seeks to answer questions about how humans ought to live and make decisions, providing a framework for assessing the consequences and moral implications of our actions. Ethical principles and theories offer guidelines for individuals and societies to navigate complex moral dilemmas and make sound moral judgments.

Ethics is a fundamental aspect of human life, playing a crucial role in personal conduct, professional behaviour, and societal values. It helps us navigate the complexities of moral choices, encourages critical thinking, and promotes consideration for the well-being of individuals and communities.

As an individual, you are responsible for defining your ethics and deciding whether you will abide by them. You are accountable for the outcomes of your decisions and the influence your ethics have on these outcomes.

A good philosophy to live by is: "Ethical behaviour is doing the right thing when no one else is watching." This partial quote from Aldo Leopold (1887-1948), an American author and philosopher, advises us to act ethically, even when we think no one is aware.

When choosing your ethics, it can be helpful to reflect on your purpose(s), values, principles, and beliefs. Consider the moral guidelines you find important in guiding your behaviour and decision-making. Think about the ethics you would like others to display when communicating or dealing with you.

Here is how the authors define their ethics (in alphabetical order):

Compassion centres around cultivating empathy, care, and concern for the well-being of others. It involves recognising the suffering and challenges faced by individuals and actively seeking to alleviate their pain or improve their circumstances. Compassion as an ethic promotes kindness, understanding, and social responsibility.

Courage requires the willingness to confront challenges, take risks, and act according to one's principles and values, even in the face of fear or adversity. It encompasses the strength to overcome obstacles, stand up for what is right, and make difficult decisions. Courage as an ethic encourages personal growth, inspires others, and contributes to positive change.

Desire to succeed involves creating a vision, defining purpose(s), and setting GOALS that add value to others. It means striving for personal and professional growth and pursuing excellence in one's endeavours. The desire to succeed as an ethic fosters determination, resilience, and a commitment to continuous learning and improvement.

Enjoyment in life involves seeking and prioritising activities, experiences, and relationships that bring joy, pleasure, and fulfilment to you, your family, friends, and everyone you interact with. It emphasises the importance of personal well-being, happiness, and the pursuit of a meaningful and enjoyable life. As we were once advised, "You only get one shot at life. Enjoy it while you can," and additionally, "Life is not a dress rehearsal, so make it count."

Financial discipline refers to the practice of managing one's financial resources responsibly and maintaining self-control in financial decision-making. It involves adopting habits and behaviours that promote financial stability, long-term sustainability, and wise use of resources. Financial discipline as an ethic can lead to improved financial well-being, reduced stress, and greater freedom to pursue personal GOALS.

Forgiveness requires the intentional act of letting go of resentment, anger, and the desire for revenge towards those who have caused harm or hurt. It is a conscious decision to release negative emotions and to extend compassion, empathy, and understanding towards oneself and others. Forgiveness promotes healing, reconciliation, and the restoration of relationships. Many people confuse this as forgiving someone else's unforgivable actions in their opinion, but we must realise that forgiveness is for us first. There is nothing more valuable than your peace of mind. If you are holding onto resentment about what someone else said, or did, or didn't do, then you are wasting your own time and creative energy. Forgive means 'to let go of completely,' which is great advice if your desire is to be wealthy.

Gratitude involves recognising and appreciating the positive aspects of life, expressing thankfulness, and acknowledging the contributions of others. It entails cultivating a sense of appreciation, humility, and mindfulness for the blessings, opportunities, and kindnesses we receive. Gratitude as an ethic fosters personal well-being, strengthens relationships, and promotes a more compassionate and interconnected world. The real test in life is to learn to be grateful for the things we perceive as 'bad;' good or bad is only in our perception, in our beliefs. If we can learn to be grateful for the tough lessons in life, we are truly learning from any perceived failures and taking full responsibility for our lives.

Goodwill encompasses a genuine desire to promote the well-being and happiness of others. It involves extending kindness, generosity, and positive intentions towards individuals and communities. Goodwill as an ethic emphasises empathy, compassion, and a commitment to creating a positive impact in the world.

Honesty emphasises truthfulness, sincerity, and transparency in our words, actions, and interactions. It involves being genuine and forthcoming in our communication, and refraining from deception, falsehoods, or misleading others.

Integrity is a fundamental and crucial ethic. It encompasses honesty, trustworthiness, and a strong moral character. It involves consistently adhering to ethical principles and behaving in a manner that is congruent with one's values, even in the face of challenges or temptations.

Respect recognises the inherent worth and dignity of individuals, as well as the diversity of perspectives and experiences. It involves treating others with consideration, courtesy, and esteem, while valuing their autonomy, rights, and boundaries. Respect forms the basis for positive and harmonious relationships, collaboration, and a just society.

Trust is the belief or confidence that someone or something is reliable, honest, and dependable. It plays a crucial role in fostering healthy relationships, cooperation, and social cohesion.

Understanding involves actively seeking knowledge, empathy, and open-mindedness to foster deeper comprehension and appreciation of others' perspectives, experiences, and ideas. It emphasises the value of empathy, curiosity, and intellectual humility in promoting mutual respect, cooperation, and constructive dialogue.

Our ethics serve as a guiding lighthouse, illuminating the path towards a wealthy mindset. They steadfastly keep us aligned with our vision, purpose(s), value creation, and GOALS, all while maintaining positive beliefs. Choose your ethics, live by them, and let them guide your decisions—avoid the rocks, and sleep well at night, every night, knowing you have given your all to every waking moment.

14 STEPS TO A WEALTHY MINDSET

STEP 6 – A HEALTHY MIND & BODY

"A healthy mind breeds a healthy body and vice versa"

– Zig Ziglar, motivational speaker

Maintaining a healthy mind and body is crucial in developing and protecting a wealthy mindset. The body serves the mind, which encompasses both our thoughts and feelings. Whether we are consciously choosing our thoughts or operating on subconscious autopilot, any manifestation of dis-ease or dis-order can significantly impact our ability to attract great wealth. The very terms "dis-ease" and "dis-order" suggest that our goal should be to maintain ease and order in our thoughts and feelings. This may take time to perfect (unless we were born to Buddhist multimillionaires!), but it is essential in our quest to attract the best into our lives. The body is a delicate instrument that responds to the thoughts and feelings held in our minds, and a change of diet alone will not help someone who refuses to work on changing their thoughts and emotions.

One of the challenges we face is the lack of a clear picture of our mind—how it works, and how we can programme (or reprogramme) ourselves. This lack of understanding makes it difficult to visualise or grasp how we can make positive changes in our health, happiness, and wealth. In our experience, most people coast through life, never realising that they have the power to make such changes.

If we asked you, "What does your mind look like?" what would you say? Most people think of their brain, but the brain isn't your mind. Your brain is part of your body; it's an electronic switching station. The mind, on the other hand, is movement, and the body is the manifestation of that movement. We've heard some fascinating descriptions of what people think their mind looks like—"a washing machine," "a scrapyard," "a roller coaster," even "white-water rapids"! You name it, and people have come up with all kinds of descriptions for their own minds.

The graphic below—Figure 1, "The Stick Man" by Dr Thurman Fleet—is a powerful visual explanation of the mind. Created in the 1930s, it was later used and taught by Bob Proctor and is now part of our teachings at Life Remixed™ seminars and training.

It's simple yet incredibly effective. We think (and visualise) in pictures, and once we understand this visual representation of the mind, we can immediately grasp the fundamental principles of self-development. We possess the power to change our thoughts on any subject at any time, which means we can also change our feelings, our behaviours, and ultimately, our results. This requires work and commitment, but the destination is well worth the journey.

Mark manifested an incurable disease and faced bankruptcy in his 30s, as documented in *Life Remixed*. The "Stick Man" graphic perfectly illustrates how ignorance and a lack of knowledge were the root causes of his problems. Once he began studying and acquiring knowledge from Bob Proctor and other self-development teachers, he developed a conscious understanding of himself. This was followed by feelings of faith, belief, and confidence, leading to well-being, expression (through books and talks), and an overall sense of being at ease.

We can all use this model to develop our life skills. The overall feeling of being at ease is what attracts business, cash flow, and ultimately wealth into our lives. This book serves as a starting point for you to understand the power that you (and all of us) have within.

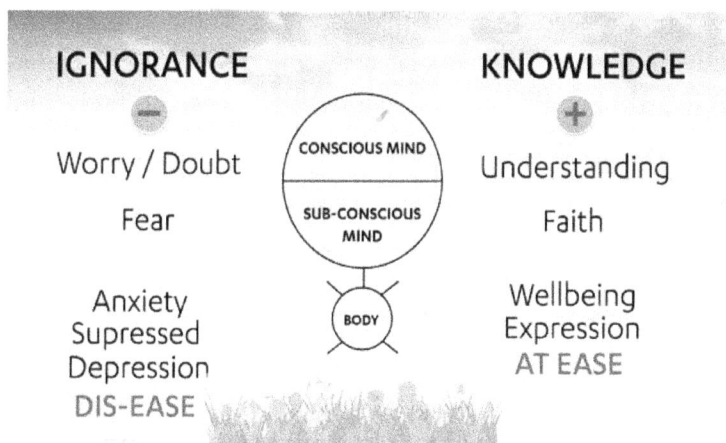

IGNORANCE   KNOWLEDGE

Worry / Doubt   CONSCIOUS MIND   Understanding

Fear   SUB-CONSCIOUS MIND   Faith

Anxiety   Wellbeing
Supressed   BODY   Expression
Depression   AT EASE
DIS-EASE

Figure 1 - 'The Stick Man' by Dr Thurman Fleet

We must understand that the word "ignorant" has often been misunderstood to mean rude, but it simply means lacking knowledge on a subject. We all possess knowledge in some areas and are ignorant in others. For instance, we are knowledgeable about self-development and the principles of success, but if you asked us to speak French, wire a house, or strip an engine, we would be completely ignorant! However, it doesn't matter much because we can hire someone who knows how to do these things. The best approach is to choose to learn, study, read, listen, and continuously grow in the subjects that interest us. Additionally, getting a coach or mentor who is already achieving what we want to achieve can accelerate our growth in the areas we want to focus on.

Part of being at ease with life involves thinking well of all, even those we believe have wronged us. Learning to find the good in everyone and understanding that each person is doing the best they can with the information they have is key. This mindset brings a peace of mind that supports a healthy mind and body, ultimately attracting success, which we define as happiness, health, wealth, including a healthy mind and body, and of course, the material items you desire.

Here are further ways in which a healthy mind and body support a wealthy mindset:

Enhanced Focus and Productivity: A healthy mind and body enable you to stay focused and productive. Regular exercise, proper nutrition, and sufficient rest improve cognitive function, memory, and concentration, allowing you to make better decisions and take actions aligned with your wealth-building GOALS.

Increased Energy and Motivation: A healthy lifestyle promotes high energy levels and motivation, which are crucial for pursuing wealthy mindset opportunities. When you feel physically and mentally strong, you are more likely to tackle challenges, persist through setbacks, and maintain the drive necessary for long-term success.

Improved Resilience: Building a wealthy mindset often involves overcoming obstacles and setbacks. A healthy mind and body foster resilience and the ability to bounce back from perceived failures. Physical fitness builds stamina and endurance, while mental well-being helps you manage stress, adapt to change, and maintain a positive outlook despite setbacks.

Better Decision-Making: A healthy mind, free from excessive stress and mental fog, allows for clearer and more rational decision-making. Good health promotes emotional stability, reduces impulsive behaviour, and enables you to analyse risks and opportunities with a calm and balanced perspective. This can prevent impulsive or emotionally driven choices that might hinder a wealthy mindset.

Increased Confidence and Self-Efficacy: A healthy mind and body can boost your self-confidence and self-efficacy. When you take care of yourself mentally and physically, you feel a sense of accomplishment, which translates into a belief in your abilities and a wealthy mindset. This confidence is valuable when it comes to taking calculated risks, seeking opportunities, and making bold moves that can lead to success.

Improved Relationships and Networking: Good health can positively impact your interpersonal relationships, which are crucial for building a wealthy mindset. When you prioritise self-care, you can engage with others more effectively, build strong professional networks, and form strategic partnerships. Healthy relationships provide valuable insights, mentorship, and opportunities for growth.

In the book *Spark* by John J. Ratey, the science of exercise and the brain is explored, offering insights on how to apply this science to a wealthy mindset. "WE ALL KNOW that exercise makes us feel better, but most of us have no idea why. We assume it's because we're burning off stress or reducing muscle tension or boosting endorphins, and we leave it at that. But the real reason we feel so good when we get our blood pumping is that it makes the brain function at its best, and in my view, this benefit of physical activity is far more important—and fascinating—than what it does for the body. Building muscles and conditioning the heart and lungs are essentially side effects. I often tell my patients that the point of exercise is to build and condition the brain."

We would also add that taking in oxygen (through deep breathing techniques and exercise that stimulates deeper breathing) can be more important than diet or even hydration. Consider this: you can go without food for a few days (or longer), without water for a couple of days, but you can only go without oxygen for a couple of minutes.

This should help you prioritise!

In *Life Remixed* Mark shares a story about overcoming rheumatic issues with his legs, back, and knees. By remixing his life and adopting a healthier mind and body approach, he dramatically improved his health. His story is worth reading to understand how these choices impacted his recovery.

A wealthy mindset involves choosing, deciding, and committing to an abundance mindset. This includes establishing your vision and purpose(s), adding value by setting clear GOALS, practising discipline, persistence, and perseverance, continuously learning and growing, and aligning your thoughts, feelings, and actions with your ethics. A healthy mind and body provide a solid foundation for cultivating these qualities, achieving success in all areas of life, and attracting the wealth you desire.

14 STEPS TO A WEALTHY MINDSET

STEP 7 – DESIRE & A POSITIVE MINDSET

"Dreams come true when desire transforms into concrete actions."

– Napoleon Hill, author

Desire and a positive mindset are two powerful factors that can greatly influence our lives and help us achieve our GOALS. Let's explore each of them in more detail:

Desire is the strong feeling of wanting or wishing for something. It acts as the driving force behind our actions and motivates us to pursue our GOALS. When we have a clear and passionate desire for something, it fuels our determination and commitment to work towards it. Desire gives us a sense of purpose and direction in life. All healthy human beings are committed to growth, and the true definition of a genius is someone who can make life pay what they would like without ever hurting another human being—something for us all to consider.

Desire is about focusing on what you want, not on what you don't want. Being able to control what you think and focusing on what you want is all part of developing a wealthy mindset.

To harness the power of desire, it's vital to:

Define your GOALS: Dream big. Then clearly identify what you desire. Set specific, measurable, achievable, relevant, and time-bound (SMART) GOALS, and take those steps towards your GOAL. When you have a clear target, it becomes easier to channel your efforts effectively.

Visualise success: Imagine yourself having already achieved your desire. Visualise the positive outcomes and the emotions associated with it. This can create a strong mental image that motivates and inspires you to act. Create a vision of your life; for instance, we have a multiple source of income map. Look at it often so it imprints on your mind, and you can get emotionally involved with the longer-term outcome.

Take consistent action: Break your GOALS into smaller, actionable steps. Consistently work towards them, even if progress seems slow at times. Patience is crucial. Maintain persistence and resilience when facing obstacles or setbacks.

A positive mindset refers to the attitude and outlook we adopt towards life's challenges and opportunities. It involves cultivating optimistic thoughts, feelings, beliefs, and attitudes, which can significantly impact our overall well-being and success.

Understand the difference between being interested and being committed to building and protecting financial wealth. A positive mindset commits.

Developing a positive mindset involves:

Positive self-talk: This is often overlooked. When Mark coaches his clients, he often hears words that the client doesn't really mean. Pay close attention to your internal dialogue and consciously choose to replace negative self-talk with positive affirmations. Encourage and support yourself, focusing on your strengths and ongoing achievements. Positive affirmations that start with "I am" and "I have," spoken with conviction, are crucial to success. In Buddhism, it's said that it's a sin to waste words. We now ensure we consciously choose our words and do our best not to waste them. Observe yourself and others (without judgment), and you'll start to see how many people waste a lot of words in their day-to-day conversations.

In *It's Not About the Money* by Bob Proctor, he discusses the importance of positivity and the process of changing your paradigm—a paradigm being defined as a multitude of habits. He emphasises shifting from "seeing is believing" to "believing is seeing." Bob rightly points out that nothing will materialise in your life unless you first believe in it. As you go about your day, it's worth considering: what are you believing about yourself right now?

Shifting away from negative thoughts and embracing positivity can be a true game-changer. It's important to recognise that some of us may need therapy to release negativity and emotional baggage, and this can be a lengthy process towards total acceptance of our current reality. However, once we've made these changes, we come to realise there is no value in worrying about problems. A wealthy mindset is a solution-oriented mindset—clearing the mental clutter from your life is incredibly powerful. Once you've helped yourself, you can then choose to help others if that aligns with your purpose.

Gratitude: Practice gratitude by acknowledging and appreciating the positive aspects of your life. Regularly reflect on what you are grateful for, as this helps shift your focus towards the good things and enhances your overall happiness. Gratitude is a muscle that builds over time, and like any muscle, it requires attention and some manageable stress and pressure to grow. The ultimate goal is to reach a place where you feel grateful for creation and life itself—for nature and the world and the ability to take your next breath. Simply say, "I am grateful," and truly feel it. This can take time to build and practice, but the result is well worth the effort.

Embrace failure as learning: Adopt a growth mindset that sees failures and setbacks as opportunities for learning and growth. Instead of dwelling on mistakes, remove or balance the emotional attachment, analyse them, extract valuable lessons, and use them to improve your future endeavours.

Paul recalls a story from a seasoned rig manager who had to spend USD 5,000 on repairs due to a genuine accident caused by one of his crew members. When asked if he planned to fire the crew member responsible for the mistake, the manager's response was unforgettable: "Of course not. I've just spent USD 5,000 training him, and I'm certain he won't make that mistake again."

Surround yourself with positivity: Surround yourself with supportive and positive-minded individuals. It's said you are the result of the five people you spend the most time with, so being in a wealthy mindset is always easier when you surround yourself with others on a similar path. Seek out sources of inspiration, such as books, podcasts, or motivational speakers, that resonate with you and uplift your spirits.

It's crucial to be mindful of the people, environments, and influences we surround ourselves with, as they can significantly impact our mindset and overall well-being.

Negative energy can drain our positivity, hinder progress, and create unnecessary stress. Nothing is more valuable than your peace of mind—it helps you create, whereas negative energy will only make you disintegrate. Here are some additional points to consider about negative people and situations:

Toxic relationships: Evaluate every relationship in your life and identify any toxic or negative influences. How do certain people make you feel? Uplifted or exhausted? Surrounding yourself with individuals who constantly bring you down, criticise your GOALS, or discourage your efforts can be detrimental to your mindset and motivation. Establish boundaries and, if necessary, distance yourself from such relationships. No one should have the power to make us *feel* anything; that must solely be our decision. However, as we go through the process of becoming financially wealthy, we must ensure we are in charge of our thoughts and feelings and not influenced negatively by others. Bob Proctor advised going on a "negativity fast," which means leaving all toxic relationships behind.

Negative environments: Take note of the environments where you spend the most time. Whether it's your workplace, social circles, or online spaces, pay attention to the overall atmosphere and how it affects your mood and mindset. Whenever possible, seek out environments that foster positivity, growth, and support. The key advice is to always start with yourself. Once you make internal changes, your outer environment will follow. If you're unhappy with your current surroundings, begin by changing your thoughts and feelings.

Media consumption: Be mindful of the media you consume, including news, social media, and entertainment. While staying informed is important, excessive exposure to negative news or engaging in toxic online interactions can contribute to a negative mindset. Consider that "negativity fast," and set limits on your media consumption, consciously choosing uplifting and inspiring content. Do this until you recognise that you are no longer viewing negative news on a regular basis and no longer emotionally triggered by it.

Self-care: Prioritise self-care and self-love practices that promote positivity and well-being. Total acceptance of yourself is the key to peace of mind. Engage in activities that bring you joy, such as hobbies, exercise, music, mindfulness, or spending time in nature. Taking care of your mental and emotional health will help you maintain a positive mindset and better cope with negative influences.

Remember, creating a wealthy mindset requires active effort and continuous self-awareness. The world is full of negativity and people with a negative mindset, and it's easy to fall into that trap. Your role is to be the difference, the creative one. People pay for good ideas, well delivered by a good person with a plan. You can be that person when you choose to be. By consciously choosing positivity and distancing yourself from negativity, you can cultivate an environment that supports your GOALS, enhances your well-being, and allows your positive thoughts to flourish and gain momentum.

Adopting and protecting a positive mindset and practising continual gratitude can indeed have a significant impact on your overall well-being. It helps you approach life with optimism and enthusiasm and allows you to appreciate the present moment. Cultivating a growing sense of gratitude is a powerful way to shift your focus towards the positive aspects of your life. Find a personal trigger, like an E-Colours wristband, which serve as a reminder to pause and reflect on what you're grateful for. Ultimately, the benefits of maintaining a positive outlook extend beyond attracting specific material things—it enhances your overall experience and allows you to embrace life with joy. Get a wristband from us at an event, or find your own trigger or anchor point and see what works best for you.

In the book *Think and Grow Rich*, Napoleon Hill describes how the Law of Attraction does not judge; it gives you what you focus on. Your dreams can come true when you focus on them, and your desire transforms them into concrete actions. The Law of Attraction in action: manifest what you want and enjoy the process.

Combining desire with a positive mindset and expressing gratitude can create a powerful synergy that propels you towards your vision, purpose(s), and GOALS in life. Your strong desire fuels your motivation, while a positive mindset helps you maintain growth and resilience, overcome challenges, and stay focused on your wealthy mindset path.

CHAPTER 6

~~~~~~~~~

14 STEPS TO A WEALTHY MINDSET

STEP 8 - SURROUND YOURSELF WITH PEOPLE OF A WEALTHY MINDSET

"The fastest way to change yourself is to hang out with people who are already the way you want to be."

– Reid Hoffman,
co-founder of LinkedIn and entrepreneur

Find someone who is living the way you would like to live and copy them. That's right, there is no giant secret here, just everything we've discussed in this book so far, and then it's about you making sound and wise decisions.

Dealing with people who do not have a wealthy mindset can indeed be draining and challenging. It's important to protect your energy and maintain your wealthy mindset, especially as you start on this journey. Often, you have to politely walk away. However, in certain situations, you may be stuck, so be prepared to deal with it in your own positive way.

Napoleon is quoted as saying, "Circumstances, what are circumstances? I create circumstances." Sometimes, this can be the hardest thing—to realise you are the creator and to take responsibility for the things you don't love about your life.

However, sometimes you cannot dictate your company, especially if you are an employee. It can feel like swimming against the tide, which creates a challenging and sometimes isolating experience. It can be disheartening when your thoughts, beliefs, or GOALS do not align with the majority in your group or community. However, it's also important to remember that someone having a different perspective can sometimes be valuable and potentially contribute to your own personal growth. Be open-minded to such differences, and you will learn from them.

Here are a few suggestions on how to navigate these situations:

Embrace your individuality: Recognise that having your own unique thoughts and perspectives is a strength. Embrace your individuality, and don't be afraid to express your opinions respectfully and confidently, keeping an open mind at all times.

Seek support: Find like-minded individuals who share your beliefs or values. This can be done through online communities, social groups, or by participating in activities related to your interests. Connecting with others who understand and appreciate your perspective can provide a sense of validation and support. Therapy and coaching are also great services when delivered by the right person for you.

Engage in respectful dialogue: When discussing your views with others who may disagree, try to engage in open-minded and respectful conversations, keeping high emotions out of the equation. Listen actively to their perspectives, and be willing to consider alternative viewpoints. Constructive dialogue can lead to mutual understanding and personal growth.

Educate yourself: Stay informed and knowledgeable about the topics that matter to you. This will help you articulate your thoughts more effectively and contribute to discussions with confidence. It may also help you find common ground or bridge gaps in understanding with others. Always seek to educate yourself on financial wealth building and protection. We should be aiming for one book per month each, on personal performance subjects.

Focus on personal growth: Use any opportunity to learn and grow as an individual. Your unique perspective can offer valuable insights and ideas. Keep developing your skills, knowledge, and talents, and strive to make a positive impact, regardless of the challenges you may face.

Maintain resilience: Swimming against the tide can be mentally and emotionally taxing. It's important to build resilience and value your well-being. Surround yourself with a supportive network, engage in self-care activities, and practise mindfulness or relaxation techniques to manage stress. Ensure you are on the right path, and you will feel passionate about what you are doing.

Remember, it's okay to be part of a group while holding different views. Embrace your authenticity and continue to pursue what you believe in. Your contributions, even if they go against the current, can make a difference in the long run. Be useful, be helpful, and always add value. Make sure you spend as much time around others who think, feel, and act in the same way.

Surrounding yourself with people who have a wealthy mindset can be incredibly beneficial for your own well-being and personal growth, especially at the start of your journey or when you need additional support in reaching your GOALS. Wealthy mindset individuals tend to have a contagious energy and belief that can uplift and inspire you to maintain a positive outlook—they are worth being around.

Here are some reasons why surrounding yourself with wealthy mindset people is important:

Support and encouragement: Wealthy mindset individuals are more likely to support and encourage your GOALS and aspirations. They can provide valuable feedback and constructive advice, and help you stay motivated during challenging times. Their positive energy can serve as a catalyst for your own personal growth.

Role models and inspiration: Being around wealthy mindset people can expose you to role models and individuals who have achieved success in various areas of life. Their stories, achievements, and positive mindset can inspire and motivate you to reach for your own GOALS and strive for success. Remember, it's okay to be inspired by someone else's journey and then create your own unique version from there. It's also vital to identify assets and liabilities in both finance and people. Listen carefully to what people are saying and doing, and make sure to connect with those who are assets to your journey.

Increased optimism and resilience: Wealthy mindset people tend to approach challenges with optimism and resilience. Their mindset and perspective can influence your own ability to bounce back from setbacks and maintain a positive outlook, even in difficult situations. Very often, they have done the hard work and are willing to share how they did it.

Healthy perspectives and constructive feedback: Wealthy mindset individuals often have a broader perspective and can offer constructive feedback in a supportive and uplifting manner. They can help you see situations from different angles, challenge limiting beliefs, and provide guidance for personal and professional growth.

To surround yourself with people of a wealthy mindset, consider the following:

Join positive communities or groups: Seek out communities, organisations, or groups that promote positivity, personal development, or shared interests. Engaging with like-minded individuals in these settings can create opportunities for meaningful connections and support. Since *Life Remixed* was first published, we have built a worldwide community of coaching clients who all support one another. Feel free to message us at hello@liferemixed.co.uk to find out more.

Expand your network: Attend events, workshops, seminars, or conferences related to your interests or GOALS. Connect with individuals who exude positivity and share similar passions or values. And always persist when pursuing what you want to achieve.

Foster existing relationships: Evaluate your current relationships and identify those individuals who consistently exhibit a wealthy mindset. Cultivate and nurture these relationships by spending quality time together, engaging in uplifting conversations, and offering mutual support.

Below you can see the characteristics displayed by those with a wealthy mindset:

1. Wealthy mindset people have a clear vision in mind.
2. They are focused on their purpose(s) in life.
3. They concentrate on creating value.
4. They set clear GOALS in life and revise their visions and purposes as needed.
5. They define and use their ethics to guide their daily decisions.
6. They take actions to maintain a healthy body and mind.
7. They create desire and maintain a positive mindset.
8. They surround themselves with like-minded people who also have a wealthy mindset.
9. They appreciate and understand the importance of diversity of thought.
10. They manage their time by prioritising tasks.
11. They manage their financial wealth.
12. They prioritise faith over fear.
13. They learn from both their successes and failures in life.
14. They continue to develop their learnings and knowledge and are never afraid to ask for help.

Remember, surrounding yourself with wealthy mindset individuals is not about seeking perfection or avoiding all challenges. It's about creating a supportive and nurturing environment that fosters your growth, resilience, and a wealthy mindset.

CHAPTER 6

⌐⌐⌐⌐⌐⌐⌐⌐

14 STEPS TO A WEALTHY MINDSET

STEP 9 – PERSONALITY DIVERSITY

*"Every individual matters, has a role to play, and
makes a difference. We do not all see and think about
life in the same way, however, leveraging personality
diversity allows us to be more accepting and to make
this world a better place."*

– Paul Grant

We would like to extend our heartfelt appreciation to Equilibria for granting us permission to reference their invaluable coaching tools on personality diversity in this book. Their dedication to understanding and promoting personality diversity has been instrumental in shaping the content within these pages.

However, it is important to emphasise that the thoughts and ideas presented here are solely our own and do not carry the official endorsement of Equilibria. While we have drawn inspiration from their methodologies, any interpretations or conclusions reached herein are independent of Equilibria.

We are immensely grateful to Equilibria for their commitment to fostering personal growth and embracing personality diversity over the last 20 years. Their resources have significantly expanded our understanding and empowered us to explore the intricacies of personality diversity.

In Chapter 4, we discussed the significance of personality diversity and its implications. In this section, we will delve into practical ways to apply this concept in your life. If you haven't yet visited the Equilibria website to complete the complimentary Personality Diversity Indicator (PDI), we encourage you to do so. It's a valuable resource that can provide further insight into your own personality style. To access the FREE PDI and learn more about personality diversity, please use the following links:

- Discover Your E-Colours (for FREE): www.equilibria. com/PDI-home
- E-Colours & Personal Intervention: www.equilibria. com/e-colors

Taking the PDI will enhance your understanding of the diverse range of personalities and help you navigate the upcoming content with a deeper perspective. However, please note that the PDI and its results are independent of this book and its authors. They are offered as a separate tool by Equilibria, and any interpretations or applications should be considered within their framework.

Whether you've already taken the PDI or plan to do so after reading this section, embracing personality diversity can profoundly impact your personal and professional growth. It opens up new possibilities for collaboration, communication, and self-awareness, ultimately enriching your journey towards a more harmonious and inclusive future. Mark credits his first E-Colours Premium Report with helping him understand himself better, enabling him to manage his strengths and potential limiters—skills that took him from bankruptcy to a six-figure salary within three years.

Personality diversity refers to the natural variation in individual personalities within a group or society. It recognises that people have different temperaments, traits, preferences, and behavioural patterns that make them unique. Just as people have physical diversity in terms of their appearance, they also exhibit psychological diversity in terms of their personalities.

Personality diversity is essential for several reasons:

Innovation and problem-solving: Individuals with different personality styles bring diverse perspectives and approaches to problem-solving. This diversity of thought can lead to more creative solutions and innovations.

Collaboration and teamwork: Personality diversity enhances collaboration and teamwork by bringing together individuals with complementary strengths and perspectives. It allows for a more balanced and comprehensive approach to achieving common GOALS.

Well-rounded decision-making: When a group consists of individuals with diverse personalities, decision-making becomes more well-rounded. Different personality styles tend to consider various factors, risks, and possibilities, resulting in more informed and balanced decisions.

Adaptability and resilience: In a rapidly changing world, personality diversity helps organisations and societies adapt and respond to new challenges. Individuals with different personalities may have varying strengths in dealing with change, uncertainty, and adversity, allowing for a more resilient collective response.

Improved understanding and empathy: Personality diversity fosters understanding and empathy among individuals. It encourages people to recognise and appreciate different perspectives, leading to more inclusive and tolerant teams and societies.

It's important to note that personality diversity should not be confused with diversity in terms of race, gender, ethnicity, or other demographic factors. While these dimensions of diversity are crucial, personality diversity focuses on individual differences in traits, behaviours, and preferences that go beyond demographic categories.

Promoting and embracing personality diversity requires an inclusive and open-minded approach that values and respects different perspectives. It involves creating environments where people feel comfortable expressing their unique personalities and ensuring that diverse voices are heard and valued.

From an E-Colours perspective, which focuses on understanding, appreciating, and leveraging personality diversity, there are distinct communication styles associated with each E-Colour or personality style. These styles can provide valuable insights into how individuals prefer to communicate and how they like to be communicated with.

Here is an overview of communication styles based on the E-Colours model:

- **Red (Doer)**: Reds tend to have a direct and assertive communication style. They prefer concise and to-the-point conversations, focusing on the bottom line. Reds appreciate clear GOALS and objectives, valuing efficiency and results. When communicating with Reds, it's best to be direct and specific, avoiding excessive detail.

- **Yellow (Socialiser)**: Yellows have an enthusiastic and engaging communication style. They enjoy lively and interactive conversations, often using storytelling and humour. Yellows appreciate positive feedback and a social atmosphere. When communicating with Yellows, it helps to be upbeat, use visual aids if possible, and emphasise the potential for collaboration and teamwork.

- **Blue (Relator)**: Blues have a calm and supportive communication style. They prefer a relaxed and harmonious atmosphere, focusing on building relationships and maintaining stability. Blues appreciate active listening and are attentive to nonverbal cues. When communicating with Blues, it's important to provide a warm and friendly environment, be patient, and show empathy and understanding.

- **Green (Thinker)**: Greens have an analytical and precise communication style. They prefer well-organised and detailed discussions, focusing on accuracy and quality. Greens appreciate logical reasoning and evidence-based arguments. When communicating with Greens, it's beneficial to provide comprehensive information, be prepared for thoughtful questions, and allow time for reflection and analysis.

You may recognise yourself in one or more of these descriptions. Equilibria has found that people tend to identify most strongly with their top two E-Colours (for example, Mark is Yellow over Red, and Paul is Red over Green). Everyone has a mix of these styles that they can access at different times.

Understanding and adapting these communication styles can enhance collaboration, minimise misunderstandings, and foster effective relationships in diverse teams. By recognising and appreciating the different preferences and needs of each personality style, individuals can tailor their communication approach to create a more inclusive and productive environment.

Here are ways you can better understand personality diversity:

Understand your strengths and the strengths of others: Recognising and understanding both your own strengths and those of others is crucial in a world that embraces and celebrates diversity. By harnessing our unique talents and capabilities, we can navigate challenges with confidence and make meaningful contributions. Understanding the strengths of others allows us to foster a culture of inclusivity and collaboration, where everyone feels valued and empowered. This understanding enables us to establish strong connections, cultivate effective communication, and embark on a collective journey of growth and success.

Understand your potential limiters and the potential limiters of others: This is a transformative journey that fuels personal and collective growth. By delving into the realm of E-Colours, we gain valuable insights into the factors that may hinder our progress or hold us back. This understanding allows us to view potential limiters as opportunities for self-improvement rather than insurmountable obstacles. Armed with this knowledge, we can take proactive steps to manage and overcome our potential limiters, unlocking our true potential and achieving success. By recognising the potential limiters of others, we cultivate empathy and compassion, extending support and encouragement as they navigate their own challenges.

Reaction vs. Response: Understanding the difference between these two can greatly impact our communication, relationships, and overall well-being. Reactions are often instinctual and immediate, while responses are consciously chosen and based on careful consideration. By cultivating the ability to respond rather than merely react, we can enhance our communication skills, deepen our relationships, and navigate challenging situations with greater ease and wisdom. The E-Colours model provides a way to understand reaction—driven by personality—versus response, which is driven by a more controlled and conscious communication.

Effective forms of recognition: Exploring effective recognition within the context of E-Colours provides a unique perspective on understanding and appreciating the predictable nature of human behaviour. By recognising and acknowledging the diverse personality styles represented by E-Colours, we unlock the transformative power of tailored recognition strategies. When we understand each individual's E-Colour combinations and their preferred communication and recognition style, we create a positive and empowering environment that fosters both personal and professional growth. Offering recognition in alignment with individuals' E-Colours taps into their intrinsic motivations, boosting their engagement, productivity, and overall well-being. Whether it's giving public praise to the outgoing and enthusiastic Yellows or offering private acknowledgement to the thoughtful, detail-oriented Greens, effective recognition becomes a catalyst for building strong, cohesive teams. By embracing the predictable nature of E-Colours and leveraging effective forms of recognition, we unlock the potential for transformative impact, where individuals and teams thrive, making collective success the norm.

When working with me: When collaborating with me, building strong working relationships becomes a shared endeavour, requiring open dialogue, empathy, and a genuine willingness to adapt to one another's needs and preferences, considering our respective E-Colours. Recognising the diverse nature of our personalities and communication styles, we can foster an environment of understanding and mutual respect. By engaging in open dialogue, we create a space where everyone feels heard and valued, enabling the exchange of ideas and perspectives. Demonstrating empathy allows us to appreciate the unique strengths and challenges each person brings to the table, cultivating a sense of camaraderie and support. Moreover, adapting to one another's needs and preferences based on their E-Colours enhances collaboration and promotes effective teamwork. By tailoring our approaches, communication styles, and problem-solving methods to align with one another's E-Colours, we foster an environment that embraces our diversity and maximises our collective potential. We can navigate challenges, leverage our strengths, and achieve shared GOALS, ultimately building strong working relationships that lay the foundation for success through the E-Colours. Some simple "do and don't" guidelines through each E-Colours lens bring such opportunities together positively.

If you want me to listen: When it comes to being heard and truly listened to, taking an E-Colours perspective can offer valuable insights into understanding individuals' listening preferences. By recognising the predictable nature of listening styles based on E-Colours, we can foster stronger relationships and optimise our interactions with others. Understanding how different E-Colours approach listening enables us to tailor our communication strategies to better engage and connect with them. For example, Reds may appreciate direct and concise communication, while Yellows may respond well to a more conversational and engaging approach. Blues may benefit from a patient and empathetic listening style, while Greens may value in-depth and thoughtful conversations. By considering these predictable patterns, we can adapt our communication to resonate with others and create an environment where they feel truly listened to and understood. In doing so, we foster stronger relationships, build trust, and optimise our interactions, enhancing collaboration and achieving more meaningful outcomes.

How to delegate to me: When delegating tasks to me, taking into account the predictable nature of E-Colour styles can guide a more structured and effective approach. By considering my specific E-Colour and its associated preferences, you can tailor the delegation process to maximise my engagement and productivity. Instructions, outlining the objectives, expectations, specific guidelines or parameters, levels of autonomy, and deadlines, all need to be given based on E-Colour requirements. You can optimise my performance, foster collaboration, and create a more fulfilling working relationship.

Leadership behaviours: E-Colour leadership behaviours emphasise the importance of tailoring leadership approaches to individuals based on their unique personality traits, preferences, and tendencies. Effective leaders recognise that each team member brings their own set of strengths and motivations, and they leverage their understanding of personality diversity to engage and motivate everyone. By taking the time to understand the E-Colours of every team member, leaders can adapt their communication styles, decision-making processes, and motivational techniques to resonate with each individual. For example, they may provide clear and concise instructions for Reds, create a positive and collaborative environment for Yellows, offer support and reassurance for Blues, and provide detailed information and logical reasoning for Greens. By customising their approach, leaders create a sense of inclusivity, foster trust, and empower team members to perform at their best. By valuing and leveraging personality diversity, leaders create a thriving and high-performing team culture where everyone feels seen, heard, and motivated to contribute their unique talents.

All this information and much more is available in the E-Colours & Personal Intervention Pocketbook, available in electronic format on Amazon, Apple, and Google Play.

And how does all this play out in financial terms?

Well, as mentioned previously in this chapter, Mark went from bankruptcy to a six-figure salary in three years by discovering that his tendencies were Yellow/Blue. With that newfound awareness, he chose to work with his strengths and manage his potential limiters. His initial Yellow/Blue report revealed that he likes people, music, and parties (if you've read *Life Remixed*, you know that he spent over 20 years as an international DJ before encountering Equilibria!). The report also noted that he could get hurt by jumping in to help someone else without thinking. In his own words, he realised there were many people like him in the world, which immediately made it okay to be himself, alleviating various anxieties. E-Colours also gave him the insight that there are many other different personality styles, meaning he needed to learn how to communicate with them if he wanted to be successful. He committed to this information, did the work, and here we are today co-writing this book. There is an important lesson here for everyone.

Paul Grant has embraced all 14 Steps to a Wealthy Mindset over the past 35 years, with the importance of personality diversity being critical to these steps. This has allowed him to reach a position within the top 0.15% of net-worth individuals, within the UK, as part of his purposes in life (see data by Frank Knight Wealth Report). Reaching this GOAL was a great achievement, but in his own words, he must continue to focus not just on maintaining this position but also to continue to grow his net worth. "Often the path is not easy, and you will face setbacks; however, treat these as learning opportunities, continue forward, and you will prevail," Paul states.

Contact Equilibria, and they can assist you with harnessing personality diversity.

www.equilibria.com/contact-us

CHAPTER 6

~~~~~~~

14 STEPS TO A WEALTHY MINDSET

STEP 10 – TIME MANAGEMENT

"Either run the day or the day runs you."

– Jim Rohn, motivational speaker

No one manages time. Time is a constant, and while we can't alter it, we can manage the tasks within it. Everyone has the same 24 hours each day, and how we perceive and use this time can vary greatly. When people claim they lack time, what they often mean is that they lack priorities.

Our perception of time can be influenced by factors like focus, engagement, busyness, procrastination, and the nature of our activities. When we're fully immersed in a task we enjoy, time seems to fly. Conversely, when we're bored or disinterested, time drags.

It's crucial to recognise that our perception of time is subjective and shaped by our mindset and emotions. By being mindful and present, we can better manage our time and make deliberate choices about how we spend it.

Equally important is avoiding the trap of becoming a "busy fool"—running around, stressed, without achieving anything of significance. You might notice many people living this way, wasting precious time.

While time itself is fixed, how we prioritise tasks and allocate time is entirely within our control.

Effective task and time management is essential for maximising productivity, achieving GOALS, and maintaining a healthy work-life balance. It involves planning, prioritising, and allocating resources efficiently to minimise stress and optimise output.

Here are key principles and strategies for effective time management:

Set Clear GOALS: Start by defining your short-term, mid-term, and long-term GOALS. Clarity in your objectives will help you prioritise tasks and allocate time effectively.

Prioritise Tasks: Identify tasks that are most profitable and potentially urgent and important, prioritising them first. The tasks that will propel you towards achieving your GOALS must be your top priority. Begin your day by reviewing your task list and use a diary or task management tool that suits you best. Some prefer a simple paper list; Paul uses a notes program that synchronises across his phone, computer, and iPad. He reviews his tasks throughout the day to keep them continually updated. Mark operates an open digital diary that his clients can book into at any time. He controls his hours by blocking off certain times to focus on business-building tasks, though as a top-colour Yellow, his passion for working with people can sometimes consume his time. Mark continually manages this and his personality style to improve his effectiveness.

Eliminate Chaos: It's easy to become overwhelmed by the multitude of tasks and responsibilities competing for our attention. However, by implementing strategies to eliminate chaos and regain control over our time, we can create a more balanced and productive life. Most people, unless they have learned to control their thoughts and feelings, experience chaotic inner lives that manifest as disorder in their external world. This can be changed through self-development and a long, patient effort in self-control.

Plan and Schedule: Create a daily or weekly schedule that allocates specific time slots for different activities. Set realistic deadlines and allow buffer time for unexpected interruptions or contingencies. Be kind to yourself if you don't complete every task; negative emotions like frustration, anger, impatience, and fear often arise unnecessarily.

Break Tasks into Manageable Chunks: Large tasks can be overwhelming, so break them down into smaller, manageable subtasks. This approach makes them easier to tackle and provides a sense of progress and achievement as you complete each one.

Avoid Multitasking: Contrary to popular belief, multitasking often reduces productivity and increases errors. Instead, focus on one task at a time, complete it, and then move on to the next.

Eliminate Distractions: Minimise distractions and interruptions. In today's digital age, we are constantly bombarded with notifications, emails, and social media updates. Consider strategies like turning off Wi-Fi and notifications, setting specific times for checking emails, and creating a designated workspace free from distractions. By establishing boundaries and protecting your time, you can maintain focus and enhance productivity.

Delegate and Outsource: Learn to delegate tasks that others can handle, freeing up your time for more critical and profitable activities. Similarly, consider outsourcing tasks that are not your strengths or require specialised expertise. For example, we outsource accounting and social media management, and we don't do our own laundry, clean our houses, or maintain our gardens. Our time is spent creating value. When you can charge a high hourly or daily rate, why spend precious hours on such tasks? Mark and his wife, Emma, even have a GOAL of hiring a cook so they can focus more on adding value, an example of super-efficient task and time management!

Practice Effective Communication: Clear and concise communication helps minimise misunderstandings, prevent unnecessary back-and-forth, and save time. Be proactive in seeking clarification, and provide clear instructions when delegating tasks. Mastering the E-Colours is a great advantage for enhancing communication.

Take Breaks and Recharge: Regular breaks are essential for maintaining focus and preventing burnout. Engage in activities that help you relax, recharge, and rejuvenate, such as exercise, meditation, or spending time with loved ones. Manage your days and weeks so that you achieve all of these while still creating value for others.

Reflect and Evaluate: Periodically review your time management practices and identify areas for improvement. Learn from past experiences, adjust your approach as needed, and adopt time-saving techniques that work best for you.

Calm Down, Speed Up: This mantra challenges the ingrained belief that being faster and stressed out equates to greater achievement. These wise words encourage us to step back, reassess our priorities, and find a balanced pace that enhances efficiency and effectiveness in the long run. By intentionally calming and slowing down, we create space for reflection, creativity, and mindfulness—key ingredients for productivity and success. It's about understanding that speed without purpose is merely spinning our wheels, while intentional calmness and sometimes adopting a steadier pace can propel us forward with greater clarity and purpose. In a world that demands constant acceleration, let's embrace the power of calmness, deceleration, and focus, and discover the remarkable results that can be achieved when we decide to calm down and speed up.

Effective task and time management is about making conscious choices on how we use the fixed time available to us. By setting GOALS, prioritising tasks, and organising our activities, we can make the most of our limited time. This approach allows us to accomplish more, achieve our GOALS, and create a balanced life. So, ask yourself: Are you running your day, or is your day running you?

CHAPTER 6

~~~~~~~~~

14 STEPS TO A WEALTHY MINDSET

STEP 11 – FINANCIAL WEALTH

"The more you learn, the more you earn."

– Warren Buffett, business magnate

Building financial wealth can appear daunting and labyrinthine to many. However, within this chapter, we endeavour to shed light on some strategies that have proven beneficial to the authors.

We will explore various topics, including:

- **Part 1 - Financial Paradigm:** Shifting Perspectives on Wealth Accumulation
- **Part 2 - Picking a Vocation in Life:** Aligning Career Choices with Financial GOALS
- **Part 3 - Law of Compensation:** Understanding the Principles of Reaping What You Sow

- **Part 4 - Reciprocity Styles**: Exploring Patterns of Give-and-Take in Financial Interactions
- **Part 5 - Investing in Yourself**: Cultivating Personal Growth as a Cornerstone of Financial Success
- **Part 6 - Financial Education**: Empowering Oneself with Knowledge About Money Matters
- **Part 7 - Creating Financial Wealth**: Strategies for Generating and Accumulating Wealth
- **Part 8 - Money**: Examining the Role and Significance of Money in Our Lives
- **Part 9 - Financial Literacy**: Developing the Skills Necessary for Financial Decision-Making
- **Part 10 - Believing Is Seeing**: Harnessing the Power of Mindset in Achieving Financial GOALS
- **Part 11 - Employee/Contractor/Owner/Investor**: Navigating Different Roles in the Economic Landscape
- **Part 12 - Multiple Revenue Streams**: Diversifying Income Sources for Stability and Growth
- **Part 13 - Assets & Liabilities**: Understanding the Distinction Between Wealth-Building and Debt
- **Part 14 - Tracking Your Financial Wealth**: Implementing Systems to Monitor and Evaluate Financial Progress
- **Part 15 - Assess Your Current Status**: Taking Stock of One's Financial Standing and Trajectory
- **Part 16 - Tax Planning**: Strategies for Minimising Tax Burdens and Maximising Efficiency
- **Part 17 - Managing & Protecting Wealth**: Safeguarding Assets and Mitigating Risks

- **Part 18 - Financial Experts**: Leveraging Professional Advice and Expertise

- **Part 19 - Safeguarding Against Compliance Practitioners**: Navigating Legal and Regulatory Frameworks Responsibly

- **Part 20 - Where Do I Start? Something to Consider**: Practical Steps for Initiating the Journey Towards Financial Well-being

Through the exploration of these topics, we aim to demystify the path to financial prosperity and equip readers with actionable insights to navigate their own wealth-building journey. Strap yourself in and enjoy.

Part 1 - Financial Paradigm: Shifting Perspectives on Wealth Accumulation

The traditional financial paradigm often encourages individuals to follow a linear path of education, employment, and retirement. It suggests that going to school, pursuing higher education, securing a job, and eventually retiring is the formula for financial success. While this paradigm has been widely accepted for many years, it is important to recognise that it may not be the only path to financial wealth in today's rapidly changing world.

In recent times, the financial landscape has become more diverse and dynamic. Alternative paths to financial success, such as entrepreneurship, freelancing, and investing, have gained prominence. The digital age has opened up new opportunities for individuals to create their own businesses, pursue their passions, and achieve financial independence.

Moreover, the concept of retirement is also evolving. Many individuals are redefining what retirement means to them, choosing to engage in fulfilling work or entrepreneurial ventures even beyond traditional retirement age. They view it as a time to pursue their interests, make a positive impact, and enjoy a balanced lifestyle. For those on the wealthy mindset journey, retirement does not even come into the equation; why would you stop doing what you enjoy?

The GOAL must be to do what you like, when you like, and with whom you like. That is what some people call retirement. But for entrepreneurs, it means you retire as soon as you find something you love, dedicate your time to get paid for, and can afford. We are only on this planet for a limited time—80 to 100 years, if we are fortunate—so we have a finite amount of time to create a wonderful life doing what we love, enjoy, or want to do.

Part 2 - Picking a Vocation in Life: Aligning Career Choices with Financial GOALS

Starting out in life, we often stumble into a vocation. Sometimes it works, but in many cases, it's a disaster. You often hear people say, "Do what you love, and the money will come." This is not advice we would give to anyone. You need to prioritise what you are passionate about, but you might not be able to make a living from it. You may need to start out by doing something you are good at; in later years, you can often move towards that passion when time and your net worth allow.

The reality is that these thought processes on picking a vocation start as young as 13 years old when you begin assessing what your future holds. Will you be able to reach this vocation? Will you enjoy it? Will you be good at it? Will it compensate you in ways that provide for your needs? These are all questions that need to be considered.

Our financial paradigm often does not consider these questions, including healthy discussions about your money needs, so as mentioned above, we need to change our paradigm.

It would be great if we could all be passionate about our vocation—whether that's being a pilot, pianist, astronaut, footballer, or tennis player—but in reality, let's at least ensure we are good at our vocation, can continually add value, and then perhaps that passion can stay alive through the years, often funded by the vocation you are good at.

If your passion cannot fund your financial needs as a vocation, then find a vocation you are good at and can add value to, one that will finance your passions. Being good at your vocation and adding value or creating multiple revenue streams are two approaches that can fund your financial needs.

Many people talk about "being lucky," but according to Paul, it's not about luck; it's about working harder and smarter than everyone else. That's a certain way to be successful in life concerning financial wealth. This book will provide you with the "smarter" parts; it's now down to you to put in that hard work. You will often see those "get-rich-quick schemes." If it looks too good to be true, it often is, so stick to working smarter and harder than the rest. This strategy worked for Paul, propelling him into the top 0.15% of wealthy net worth individuals in the UK.

When asking Paul about working smarter, he explained this with some examples. His initial push to become an expat employee back in 1997 was based on several factors, including (a) reducing his tax liability by at least 20%, (b) reducing his housing expenses by 10%, and (c) increasing his revenue streams by 10% by renting out his UK property. This resulted in a 40% positive swing in financial wealth. This concept was also something he applied when starting his own company and deciding where he wanted to live in the world, which added a further 50% in cost-of-living savings, a 70% reduction in company admin expenses, and an optimised tax position contributing to a 40% saving in personal tax exposure. He was able to increase his ability to add to his financial wealth by multiple factors when combining this with added revenue streams. According to Paul, it's important to consider both revenues and costs when optimising your financial wealth positions.

Recent changes in the Thailand tax laws and thinking in advance about your options is another example of thinking smarter. This law was announced in September 2023 and commenced in January 2024. This thought process and implementation included considering various options or combinations: (a) bringing in cash prior to the new regulations, (b) using Singapore credit cards to minimise cash purchases in Thailand while managing this process without creating a debt mentality, (c) contingency planning with the option to sell locally stored gold bullion, (d) tax-free gifting to his son, (e) tax-free gifting to his partner, (f) the option to legally import cash during your travels into the country, and (g) what existing cash could still be a possibility for legally bringing into the country after the regulations are in place. Most people tended to talk about the new tax laws but did nothing to optimise their position. This comes down to the attitude of being INTERESTED vs COMMITTED and working smarter with your environment to optimise your tax position.

Part 3 - Law of Compensation: Understanding the Principles of Reaping What You Sow

The law of compensation is also worth researching. What you are compensated for financially in this life is in direct result of the need for what you do, your ability to do it, and the difficulty in replacing you. Ralph Waldo Emerson once wrote an essay titled "Compensation" that was first published in 1841. In his work, Emerson reflects on the concept of compensation, or the idea that there is a balance or reciprocity in life that ensures that we receive what we give. He suggests that everything in the universe operates according to this principle, and that every action has an equal and opposite reaction. He goes on to suggest that individuals who understand this principle and live their lives in accordance with it will experience a sense of balance and fulfilment, while those who do not will experience frustration and disappointment. "Compensation" is considered one of Emerson's most important works and is widely regarded as a seminal text in American literature. The essay is often studied as an expression of Emerson's philosophical beliefs about the interconnectedness of all things and the importance of living in harmony with the universe.

Part 4 - Reciprocity Styles: Exploring Patterns of Give-and-Take in Financial Interactions

Your reciprocity style is the foundation for building and protecting financial wealth. Become a "Successful Giver"—not a doormat. Understanding the difference can be the making of you. This is what we find most magnetic about Successful Givers: they get to the top without cutting others down, finding ways of expanding the pie that benefit themselves and the people around them.

Successful Givers advance the world, whereas takers advance themselves and hold the world back. Observe and be careful who you surround yourself with on your journey.

Give and Take, by Adam Grant, presents the fascinating secrets to givers' success. The results are unequivocal: givers gain big. Jack Welch, Richard Branson, Jon Huntsman Sr.—all of them are givers. In a world in which so many takers, such as Bernard Madoff and Raj Rajaratnam, have ruined lives and reputations, this book will reassure readers that the real power lies in becoming a giver. Since most people aren't born givers, Grant not only presents the case for why givers win, but he also offers their hidden strategies for winning.

Part 5 - Investing in Yourself: Cultivating Personal Growth as a Cornerstone of Financial Success

Think about this: if you can't or don't invest in yourself, why should or would anyone else invest in you? Many employees get stuck here; they get a job, stay in their comfort zone, don't grow or invest in themselves, and never realise their potential to become great.

Purely as an observation, the majority of financial issues come from a lack of investment, either individually or in society, combined with negative money beliefs and a general fear of not being enough or having enough. Work on these fears, and your whole life will improve.

You need to start by investing in yourself by making the time to start your education today. Put aside some time and money and work out how you can maximise this benefit. For example, Paul subscribes to certain magazines, books, and audiobooks, and has a one–two hour slot each day in his schedule where he invests in himself by learning more about creating and maintaining financial wealth. There are suggested books and subscriptions included in this book that you could use as your starting point.

Part 6 - Financial Education: Empowering Oneself with Knowledge About Money Matters

All that has been said so far might sound daunting to many, and you will, of course, make all your own decisions in your life. However, do not be put off; there are people around you to help you understand by explaining such issues. This book contains a lot of help about how to start managing your finances, and we have success coaching and coaches available to help further.

Be prepared to embark on a lifelong learning process.

Embrace knowledge and growth as part of a wealthy mindset, and you can enhance your knowledge and skills through various resources. These could include magazines, newspapers, financial education programmes, workshops, online courses, books, and seeking advice from coaching and financial professionals. By developing financial literacy, you can gain control over your finances, make informed decisions, and work towards achieving your short-term and longer-term financial GOALS and overall financial wealth.

Reading the *Harvard Business Review*, *The Economist*, and *Forbes* can provide you with valuable insights into various aspects of business, management, strategy, and financial information. Here's a brief overview of what you can expect from each publication:

1. ***Harvard Business Review*** (HBR): HBR is a renowned publication known for its in-depth articles on business and management. It covers a wide range of topics, such as leadership, innovation, strategy, organisational behaviour, marketing, and more. HBR articles are often research-based and provide practical insights and frameworks that can be applied in real-world business scenarios.

2. ***The Economist***: This weekly international publication covers a broad range of topics, including economics, politics, technology, and global affairs. It offers analysis and commentary on global business trends, economic indicators, and provides valuable insights into the implications for businesses and industries worldwide.

3. ***Forbes***: A prominent business magazine, *Forbes* focuses on business news, entrepreneurship, leadership, and finance. It covers a wide range of industries and provides articles on various business-related topics, including industry trends, market analysis, financial advice, and profiles of successful entrepreneurs and business leaders.

In addition to these publications, you may also consider exploring other reputable sources such as *Bloomberg*, *Financial Times*, *Wall Street Journal*, and the *McKinsey Quarterly*. These publications can provide you with diverse perspectives and keep you informed about the latest developments in the business world.

Actively reading, learning, absorbing, and critically evaluating the information you take in is crucial for developing a well-rounded understanding. Seeking out different viewpoints allows you to gain diverse perspectives and challenge your own assumptions. Exploring specialised publications relevant to your interests or industry can provide you with targeted insights and expertise.

Furthermore, embracing a wealthy mindset involves recognising the importance of continuous learning and seeking assistance when needed. Financial literacy is a valuable skill set, and it's perfectly acceptable to ask for help or guidance in areas that may be unfamiliar to you. Building a supportive network of individuals who are knowledgeable about finance can provide you with valuable insights, advice, and resources to enhance your financial literacy.

Remember, financial literacy is a lifetime journey, not a short sprint. It's essential to stay curious, remain open-minded to learning, and always seek guidance whenever necessary.

While education remains valuable, it is essential to recognise that it is not limited to formal schooling or university degrees. Additionally, there is an entire school of thought that the current educational system doesn't prepare children for life with any (or very little) real-life training, in subjects like how to understand ourselves and each other, how to make a relationship work, how to make money, how to create a business, how to be healthy, etc. This is where lifelong learning, acquiring new skills, and adapting to emerging trends are crucial in today's rapidly changing job market.

It is important for you to critically examine the traditional financial paradigm and consider alternative paths that align with your vision, purpose(s), and GOALS. Taking calculated risks, embracing innovation, and being open to lifelong learning can lead to greater financial fulfilment and success in today's diverse and ever-evolving financial landscape. A wealthy mindset is all about making good decisions and capitalising on these opportunities.

When we talk about "the new financial paradigms," consider some interesting takeaways from *Rich Dad Poor Dad* by Robert Kiyosaki, which is certainly worth a read as part of your learning journey. Consider the following:

1. **We All Need Financial Education**: Most students leave school with zero financial skills. They learn how to get a job but have no idea how to make more money from their own money or how to spend money wisely. You need to educate yourself financially to take charge of your money. Money makes a great servant but a terrible master. Money is a tool and makes you more of what you already are.

2. **The Difference Between Rich and Poor Is Priority**: Rich people's priorities are needs/investments/wants, and poor people's priorities are often wants/needs/investments.

3. **Change Yourself**: Accept that you are the problem, and stop blaming others. Responsibility is the key to freedom. When you understand you are the problem and start to make changes, your environment and financial results will start to change. Mark wrote about this in *Life Remixed*.

4. **How to Change**: Read every day, study successful people, get into action, quit a bad habit, replace it with a good habit, increase your skills, overcome fear, have belief and faith in yourself, build confidence, get out of your own way, get out of your comfort zone, stay focused with a success list, write a letter to your future self, and always learn from people who inspire you. Keep an open mind on all subjects at all times. Work with a Success Coach to accelerate your journey.

5. **Use Accounting to Keep Your Money**: Assets put money in your pocket; liabilities take money out of your pocket. Rich people acquire assets, poor people acquire liabilities.

6. **Your Mind Is Your Most Valuable Asset**: Train your mind to always see opportunity, leverage money from multiple sources, and organise intelligent and focused people to add value to as many people as you can serve.

7. **Become a Generalist Rather Than a Specialist**: Specialisation is for salary, not for the big money, so always work to learn, not to earn. The money will follow.

Part 7 - Creating Financial Wealth: Strategies for Generating and Accumulating Wealth

There is a difference between creating financial wealth and maintaining/managing financial wealth, and you need to be aware of these differences.

Building significant financial prosperity does not depend on charging for your time; rather, it hinges on the value you generate. Instead of invoicing based on hours, set your prices based on the value you provide. Developing mastery of business skills will lead you to financial success. By honing your business acumen, you have the potential to create substantial financial wealth in your life. This is one of the most important pieces of advice that will set you on the path to substantial financial wealth: never stop developing your business skills. These will allow you to open your mind and develop the ideas and opportunities that will come your way. If you have an idea but little or no business acumen, then you will be reliant on others to help develop this idea into a profitable business. People pay for good ideas, so do as much as you can each day to develop your mind, and you will always create ideas and attract amazing clients into your life. Once you have too many clients, that is when you call in others to support you.

Becoming an expat was a great first step for Paul in creating financial wealth. He reduced his tax exposure, and many of his expenses were covered by the company he worked for, such as travel and housing. In his first year in 1997, he put USD 40,000 into investments, did not have to pay for accommodation or cars, and gained from renting his UK property. This was driven by the opportunity that he took the time to notice and push his career in that direction. It would have been easy to stay in the UK, but the expat route offered these financial gains. That does not mean to say that everyone needs to be an expat to create financial wealth. What it does mean is that you need to be aware of your surroundings and look for opportunities, which can come in the form of multiple revenues from side hustles, a shift in career path, promotions, or debt reductions. Look around you, and search for these opportunities.

Part 8 - Money: Examining the Role and Significance of Money in Our Lives

Money is a recognised and essential tool in modern society that serves as a medium of exchange for goods and services. It holds significant influence and impact on various aspects of our lives, including our livelihoods, lifestyles, and opportunities. However, money itself is a neutral entity; it is either paper in your pocket, numbers on a plastic card, or figures on a screen in front of you. It is the values, beliefs, and actions associated with money that shape its impact and its ability to be used as a medium of exchange.

Money can be a means to meet our basic needs, provide security, and enable us to pursue our vision, purpose(s), and GOALS. It allows us to access education, healthcare, housing, and other resources that contribute to our financial wealth. Additionally, money can facilitate experiences, leisure activities, travel, and personal enrichment.

Money is often a subject that many people stress about and shy away from, with the exception of those with a wealthy mindset, who openly share their thoughts on money and how to harness its true value. Make that transition, and start to be more comfortable talking about money. Practice makes permanent, and repetition is mastery. Understand that poor people don't talk about money, generally through fear. You may remember your parents saying it's rude to talk about money (Mark does). Well, that is a mistake and will keep you poor. Financially wealthy people do talk about money, and they're perfectly comfortable with it. Truly financially wealthy people do not do this in an egotistical way; they discuss money simply without emotion and in a very matter-of-fact way, similarly as they would any other tool in their toolbox. Financially wealthy people talk about and use money as a tool and enjoy the fair exchange.

However, the pursuit of money can also have its challenges and potential pitfalls. The relentless pursuit of money without consideration for other aspects of life, such as relationships, personal wealth, and societal impact, can lead to imbalance and dissatisfaction. It is crucial to maintain a healthy mental perspective on money and strive for a wealthy mindset that includes financial wealth rather than being solely focused on accumulating money. Our thoughts and emotions can have a huge impact on our outcomes around money. As Bob Proctor taught us, "Money makes you more of what you already are," and he was right. We all know of people who seem nice when they're poor, but when they make (or win) a lot of money, they go the opposite way. The truth is, in that instance, they were never a particularly good person in their thoughts and emotions before, and the money arriving just made them more of what they already were. We can also think of lottery winners whose minds are not prepared for the big win; they may feel unworthy of such a large amount of money, and within 12 months, all the money is gone, and they are back to square one—or in some cases, even worse off. We know of these stories as they are the ones that make the headlines.

Indeed, the much healthier perspective of money as a tool for circulation, rather than mere accumulation, is gaining recognition. Viewing money as a means of circulation emphasises its potential to create value and contribute to the economy and society as a whole. Instead of focusing solely on accumulating money, this perspective encourages individuals to engage in financial transactions that foster economic growth, innovation, and positive social impact. Mark likes the story that if we observed a troop of monkeys, and one of the monkeys kept all the nuts and stockpiled them for itself, not sharing with the rest, we might observe and say that monkey had some potential mental problems. However, when a human does the same with money, we put them on the front of *Forbes* magazine and celebrate them! This added a light-hearted perspective, of course. In addition, Paul adds to not allow this circulation of money as an excuse for overspending; there must be a balance in both, when to circulate and when to accumulate. For example, if you look at gold as an investment, if it's something that you view as part of your portfolio, you circulate money to buy on a regular basis and then accumulate the gold long term to take advantage of its long-term gain. That monkey with the potential mental problems could be simply getting ready to buy gold, so possibly we can be too quick to judge the actions of others. The monkey story has another layer, too. What if all the other monkeys were very lazy and decided not to spend time collecting nuts? Does that mean they are entitled to share in the "mental monkey's" efforts? Does that mean others have an entitlement to share in your gains when not contributing? In capitalism, we all have a responsibility to improve ourselves in the service of others. However, some choose not to or, indeed, are unable to. There are sometimes many sides to a story, but the issue of "entitlement" is one of the main challenges Paul has faced in the last 35 years, where many think they have an entitlement to share in his success while doing nothing to contribute.

When money circulates, it flows through various economic activities, such as purchasing goods and services, investing in businesses, and supporting charitable endeavours. This circulation stimulates economic activity, creates jobs, and distributes wealth, ultimately benefiting individuals and communities.

It is also important to recognise that money is a tool that can create positive change and contribute to the financial wellbeing of others. Philanthropy, charitable giving, and supporting causes that resonate with our values can provide a sense of purpose and fulfilment beyond personal financial gain. Money is energy, attracted by your thoughts, feelings, and actions—your wealthy mindset. Those who manage their thoughts and emotions effectively attract money through creativity and by nurturing ideas based on solid foundations, with the support of others.

Ultimately, our relationship with money is deeply personal and varies greatly among individuals. It's crucial to reflect on our vision, purpose(s), and GOALS to establish a healthy and balanced relationship with money—one that aligns with a wealthy mindset and enables us to lead fulfilling lives while making a positive impact on ourselves, others, and society.

Our filter on money—or indeed on any subject—is our belief system, programmed by parents, teachers, society, and other influences, starting when we're young and not able to have our own cognitive thoughts. When we're children, we only pick up on vibrations—mad, bad, sad, or glad vibes from those around us—and as we grow up, we do get the chance to ultimately decide for ourselves the answer to the question, "Is this a friendly universe?" However, from childhood, this has often been decided for us in advance, so it takes time, effort, and study to change it. In Life Remixed™ Coaching, we often talk a lot about taking responsibility. We cannot blame those who brought us up (although we often spend many years doing so) for our weaknesses. When the moment comes and we decide that taking full responsibility truly is the key to freedom, and we take full responsibility for our own financial outcomes—however we came into this world—that is the moment we start to move towards a wealthy mindset. I'm sure we'd all love to have been born into this world to peaceful Buddhist multimillionaires, but neither of us was, so there was, and is, always work to be done.

Part 9 - Financial Literacy: Developing the Skills Necessary for Financial Decision-Making

Financial literacy encompasses the knowledge and skills required to make informed and effective decisions about personal finances. It includes understanding key financial concepts like budgeting, saving, investing, managing debt, and planning for the future. Developing financial literacy is essential for achieving financial wealth and making sound financial choices that align with a wealthy mindset.

Here are some key components of financial literacy:

1. **Budgeting**: Creating a budget involves tracking income and expenses to ensure that spending aligns with financial GOALS. It helps individuals prioritise their spending, save for future needs, and avoid excessive and unmanageable debt. Make a budget, continually review it, and follow it.

2. **Saving and Investing**: Financial literacy includes understanding the importance of using money as a tool and the different investment options available to you. Learning about concepts like compound interest, risk management, and diversification can help individuals make informed decisions when it comes to saving and investing for the future.

3. **Debt Management**: Financial literacy involves understanding the different types of debt, interest rates, and repayment strategies. It helps individuals make responsible borrowing decisions, avoid excessive debt burdens, and manage existing debts effectively.

4. **Understanding Credit**: Financial literacy includes knowledge of and managing credit scores, credit reports, and how credit works. Understanding these concepts allows individuals to build and maintain good credit, which can impact their ability to secure loans, mortgages, or favourable interest rates.

In the UK, we have plenty of credit services available, and 68% of adults use credit cards and 22% have mortgages (Google source), so it's not exactly a small number. According to Mark, we've been taught that credit is bad, and we should avoid it at all costs. If you've read Robert Kiyosaki's book *Rich Dad Poor Dad*, you'll understand that this is "Poor Dad" thinking. If you think of hugely wealthy people that you know of, many leverage as much credit as they can handle, again using money as a tool and not having emotional attachments to the money or the outcome. "Rich Dad" thinking requires us to think as entrepreneurs and business leaders, and even if you are a very risk-averse person, there are still routes for you to leverage finance to develop your idea or business.

Paul's view is that debt is a very risky situation to put yourself into, and many lose control of their ability to manage their finances. Using property, as shown in *Rich Dad Poor Dad*, works, but it's how you build this as part of your portfolio. Using property to build financial wealth is not a bad idea; it's how you manage this process. There are many examples where people get over-leveraged in credit and lose everything. That's not managing your finances; it's a form of gambling where the odds are stacked against you. Recall what happened in the housing crisis, during COVID, and more recently when rates increased dramatically. Credit providers are there to make money from consumers, instilling a sense of greed and entitlement for the consumer, and they are not your friends.

Mark and Paul have differing views on credit scores. Paul says, "Forget about your credit scores; being debt-free is the safe way to build wealth in a controlled way." *Baby Steps Millionaires* by Dave Ramsey is a great example of this. Mark says, "Leverage responsibly where you can, and use the capital wisely to invest and build wealth." This may well be because of their differing personality styles and experiences.

Paul has a young son with his wife, but this has only been over the last 8 to 15 years. He has been utilising the wealthy mindset steps for 35 years, and he discounts this as influencing his approach to financial wealth building. It has been 27 years since Paul last had a car payment, and 24 years since he last had a mortgage, showing that the impact of his wife and child has not influenced his approach. Mark and Emma, his wife, do not have children, and this is one of the reasons Mark states as their reason for using credit opportunities.

Both use different approaches, and the approach you choose depends on your perspective and money beliefs. Paul's response to this is, "If you want to gamble your financial wealth, then use credit and leverage as much as you can; even consider a trip to the casino. However, if you want to manage your finances, then avoid credit and build your wealth in a controlled way where you decide on the conditions."

5. **Financial GOAL Setting**: Financial literacy helps individuals set both challenging and stretching financial GOALS and then develop strategies to achieve them. This includes saving for major purchases and establishing an emergency fund. It's important that you include this in your financial GOALS, have these in writing, and continually review your progress. What you focus on is

what gets done. You can start small if this helps you start to believe in yourself, especially when you achieve it.

You could start by saying to yourself, "I am so happy and grateful now that I have [amount] of unexpected income in the next three months," and then get to work. You'll be surprised how many further opportunities arise when you work your mind into a higher vibration.

You do need to create an emergency fund; some say three to six months, others like one year. COVID certainly showed the value of this. Sixty percent of Paul's net worth can be turned into cash within a matter of days without taking a loss on the initial principal invested, creating a larger-than-needed emergency fund. This obviously excludes any property or company investments, where it takes longer to convert such assets. That helps him relax and create during the day by having access to funds and sleep well at night knowing he can manage any financial uncertainties.

In addition, Mark has been able to create a financially wealthy life by following similar strategies of relaxation and creativity. This started by choosing faith over fear (this was a huge effort in self-development to achieve), then learning to add value to every person and every situation, and creating multiple companies and multiple sources of income while setting and achieving financial goals, all of which in his stressed-out younger life he was unable to clearly understand or create.

6. **Risk Management**: Financial literacy encompasses understanding and managing financial risks, such as

insurance coverage for health, property, and life. It involves evaluating risks and choosing appropriate insurance options to protect against unexpected events.

7. **Consumer Awareness**: Financial literacy includes being informed about consumer rights, understanding financial products and services, and making informed choices as a consumer. This knowledge empowers individuals to make wise purchasing decisions and avoid scams or fraudulent schemes.

8. **Long-term Financial Planning**: Financial literacy involves considering long-term financial needs, such as retirement planning and estate planning. It includes understanding retirement accounts, investment vehicles, and strategies for wealth preservation and transfer. It's never too early to get started on wills, inheritance tax planning, and trusts.

9. **Tax Planning**: Financial literacy involves considering tax optimisation, tax avoidance, and tax evasion, all of which are very different aspects of tax planning. Tax evasion is, of course, illegal, with serious consequences for those found guilty, from financial penalties to criminal conviction and imprisonment. You don't want to go anywhere near tax evasion. Always stay on the right side of the law.

10. **Tax Optimisation**: This can be where you make tremendous gains. In the UK, we pay 45% in the top tax bracket along with 20% VAT. This was part of Paul's plans over 27 years ago when he opted to become a non-UK resident and optimise his UK tax position. That does not mean to say that you must be a non-resident to make financial wealth; you should, however, be aware of where you can optimise your tax position.

Part 10 - Believing Is Seeing: Harnessing the Power of Mindset in Achieving Financial GOALS

It's important to protect your mind from negative influences. Even during difficult times or recessions, there are still people who make millions. If you watch the mainstream news, you'll very rarely hear about someone's successes—unless they win the lottery, of course! Only allow positive influences into your mind until you can deal with the mass negativity of the world and not get emotionally involved with it.

"Believing is seeing" offers a new paradigm to many. You may well have heard, "I'll believe it when I see it," before. This is a popular phrase from a negative mindset point of view and also shows a real lack of knowledge of how our minds actually work. We must take control of our thoughts and feelings before we can really visualise all the money we want to make. Once we visualise positively, we can feel how enthusiastic we are for life and how happy we will be to achieve the GOAL. Deciding what you will do with the money before you set your financial GOAL is a powerful thing. Tony Robbins has said, "In order to succeed, you need desperation or inspiration"—sometimes both! Imagine what it's like to fly business or first class every time, to drive that Porsche, Bentley, Aston Martin, or McLaren, or to wear those new designer clothes and handbags. Paul often refers to this as guilt-free spending. Forget about what average looks like; let it go. You need—no, you MUST—think big and remember that Nike slogan: JUST DO IT!

Paul revised his financial GOALS over 26 years ago in Thailand. His initial GOALS were to purchase a nice, small car (Toyota Vios), a nice small home (two bedrooms with a small pool), and with investments of USD 500,000, he could stop working. Then his paradigm changed; he started to think bigger, and he is now way beyond those initial GOALS, having an absolute ball every day.

Part 11 - Employee/Contractor/Owner/Investor: Navigating Different Roles in the Economic Landscape

Where do you see your role now, and what do you want to progress towards?

As an Employee: Your primary focus may be on earning a consistent income through regular employment. However, you are really limited in how you can progress your financial wealth. We are not saying it's impossible to grow, only that it's limited, as an abundance of your time is dedicated to your employer and a lot of your income is taken in tax. There are times when a steady payment and some security from an employer are useful. However, if we believe we have security only from our job—with a mentality of "just over broke"—then we are missing the point. Post-COVID, a side hustle is also a good idea.

As a Contractor: Contractors often have more flexibility and autonomy in their work but also face additional responsibilities, such as managing their own taxes, invoicing, and obtaining clients. Understanding how to set appropriate rates, budget for variable income, and navigate self-employment taxes is crucial. Financial discipline, including saving for taxes and establishing an emergency fund, can provide stability and security as a contractor. Additionally, investing in professional development and networking can help expand your client base and enhance your earning potential.

As an Owner: As a business owner, financial literacy becomes even more critical. Managing cash flow, monitoring expenses, and understanding financial statements are essential to the success of your business. Effective financial planning, including setting business GOALS, budgeting, and strategising for growth, can help you make informed decisions and maximise profitability. It is also important to separate personal and business finances and to have a contingency plan in place to weather national and international economic fluctuations. Here, the majority of your time is very much dictated by your own business.

As an Investor: This is the ultimate GOAL. Investing involves putting your money to work to generate returns over time. Whether you are investing in company ownership, stocks, bonds, property or real estate, gold, silver, whisky, watches, cars, or other asset classes, understanding risk tolerance, diversification, and long-term investment strategies is key. Conducting research, staying informed about market trends, and seeking advice from financial professionals can help you make informed investment decisions aligned with your financial GOALS and risk appetite. The great thing about being an investor is you make recurring money while you are sleeping. Always consider what makes you sleep well at night when choosing your investments. Balancing your portfolio is another one of those things that helps you do that.

Throughout Paul's journey, he encountered a significant obstacle when he found himself stuck in an employee role over two decades ago. However, thanks to his now business partner Dean Masters' unwavering support and the fortuitous Equilibria opportunity, he managed to break free from that stagnant position. This breakthrough propelled him towards new paths, leading him to embrace roles as a contractor, owner, and investor, which he finds himself comfortably situated in today. Nevertheless, we both understand that the future is unpredictable, and our circumstances may evolve once again. Yet, one constant that will remain unwavering is our commitment to maintaining a wealthy mindset, no matter what. Regardless of the roles we assume or the ventures we undertake, we will continue to cultivate and grow a wealthy mindset that prioritises financial wealth, growth, and abundance for all.

It's essential to recognise that different individuals have varying aspirations and preferences when it comes to their careers. While some people may find fulfilment and purpose as employees, others may be drawn to entrepreneurial ventures or investment opportunities. In the case of Paul's son, Jack, who is over nine years old as we write, it is never too early to start a wealthy mindset. Jack's current passion for flying passenger airplanes suggests that being an employee or contractor in the aviation industry could align with his ambitions.

As you discuss your child's, partner's, or even friends' passions with them, it's crucial to emphasise that following a wealthy mindset doesn't limit your or their options. Being an employee or contractor doesn't preclude you from pursuing investment opportunities or exploring ownership possibilities. In fact, once you have mastery of yourself, it's important to show others that a wealthy mindset encompasses a holistic approach to financial wealth, encompassing multiple avenues for wealth creation that can often run in parallel with employment or contractor opportunities.

We encourage everyone to remain open-minded and flexible, understanding that your preferences and GOALS may evolve over time. By instilling in others the idea that you have the power to change directions and pursue new opportunities as they arise, you can empower yourself and others to make informed choices aligned with your vision, purposes, and GOALS. Regardless of your chosen path, reinforcing the notion that a wealthy mindset embraces the concept of continuous learning, adapting, and seeking opportunities will serve you well in your journey towards financial success.

Part 12 - Multiple Revenue Streams: Diversifying Income Sources for Stability and Growth

Having multiple revenue streams or multiple sources of income is an effective strategy for building wealth and financial security. It involves generating income from various sources, which reduces reliance on a single income stream and provides a more diversified and resilient financial foundation. We read something recently indicating that millionaires and multimillionaires had, on average, at least seven multiple revenue streams. Mark indicates that, currently looking at both his and Emma's personal multiple revenue streams, they have at least ten different income areas, some of which can generate several streams of income. When one lowers, another will pick up. Paul indicates that he currently has around 15 different revenue streams.

Here are a few key benefits of having multiple revenue streams:

1. **Risk Mitigation**: Relying solely on one source of income can leave you vulnerable to financial setbacks if that source is disrupted or lost. By diversifying your

income streams, you spread the risk and minimise the impact of any individual loss. If you have all the proverbial "eggs in one basket" or think security lies in your job alone, work to change that as soon as possible. Begin to establish something else outside of work that could sustain you if, for example, you were asked to leave your job. We read something interesting recently: "Your job is only paying you as they can't get it done any cheaper at the moment." That may be a cynical view, but there will be people who approach life like that, and some of them run companies. Your income is your responsibility, no one else's. Do not allow someone else to take responsibility for you. Always remember, taking responsibility is the key to your freedom.

2. **Increased Income Potential**: Different revenue streams offer different income potential. By exploring various avenues, such as entrepreneurship, investments, rental properties, freelance work, or royalties, you can tap into additional income streams and potentially increase your overall earning potential. Remember, life is short, and you deserve to be happy. Make sure you are living life as an adventure and getting the maximum out of your experience.

3. **Flexibility and Adaptability**: Multiple revenue streams provide flexibility and the ability to adapt to changing circumstances. If one income stream becomes less profitable or no longer aligns with your GOALS, having alternative sources can help you pivot and explore new opportunities.

4. **Wealth Accumulation and Financial Growth**: By generating income from multiple sources, you can accelerate your wealth accumulation efforts. Each revenue stream contributes to your overall financial growth, allowing you to save, invest, and build assets more effectively.

To create multiple revenue streams, start considering exploring various avenues such as starting a side business by looking at what you are good at or passionate about, investing in stocks, real estate, or other assets, monetising your additional and potentially transferrable skills through freelancing or consulting, creating and selling digital products or services, or exploring passive income opportunities like royalties or affiliate marketing. For example, sharing your experience of a good idea, product, or service has value to companies, and a good ethical company will offer you a percentage return on business you bring in.

Mark encourages people to understand and set income GOALS. It takes time and patience to achieve, but he is always working on passive income streams. For him, this means property investment and growing other business ventures. You must understand and appreciate the difference between passive and active income. Active income is generated from tasks linked to your job or career that take up your time. Passive income, on the other hand, is income that you can earn with relatively minimal effort, such as renting out a property or earning money from a business without much active participation. As we grow older gracefully, passive income must become part of your overall GOALS. Think on this for a while, and then start taking action.

In the realm of ambitions and dreams, the meeting of passion and prosperity casts a spell of happiness. To envision a life where your deepest passions create seamlessly with financial gain is a wonderful notion, brimming with promise and fulfilment. For Mark and Paul, the flame of ambition burns brightly in the pursuit of making money, not only for themselves but also for their friends, family, colleagues, and clients. It is passion that propels them forward, guiding their steps along the path of entrepreneurship, investment, and wealth creation. They continually visualise their futures with unwavering dedication to their vision, purposes, and GOALS that align in harmony with the growth of their financial prosperity. The continued joy received from doing what they love is mirrored by the rewards it brings. In this realm of possibilities, they are not confined by the limitations of conventional employment, the job—the "just over broke" situation that can develop—but instead are empowered by the limitless potential of their own ventures. And in their continuing journey of attracting success, they not only carve their own path but also endeavour to uplift others—those who are committed, that is—leaving those people with the impression of increase from their involvement in a project, openly sharing the results of their efforts, and spreading the wealth to those who have journeyed alongside them. In this life of passion and profit, where money is a combination of circulation and accumulation, they find a rhythm that resonates with both of them, which continues to attract a future where their greatest joy and financial abundance continue hand in hand.

However, it's important to note that managing multiple sources of income and revenue streams requires creative thinking, careful planning, organisation, monitoring, action-taking, and time management. In the last two decades, we have thought very carefully about our capacity and when the time is right to add a new revenue stream and stop a venture. Paul commented that he can think of at least five major revenue-generating incomes that they decided to step back from. "Sometimes you have to make such decisions to keep moving forward."

Ultimately, having multiple sources of income and revenue streams can provide financial stability, open up new opportunities, and contribute to long-term wealth creation. For someone who is passionate about giving great service, adding value, and making money, it's one of the fundamentals of a wealthy mindset that develops as part of the process.

In his story, Paul highlighted the significance of cultivating multiple revenue streams, which played a pivotal role in his transition into entrepreneurship. He nurtured a diverse array of over 15 revenue streams at any one time over the years, each representing a unique opportunity for growth and prosperity. It was akin to tending a garden, watching it develop and flourish with each new source of income. These revenue streams served as the foundation of his entrepreneurial success, enabling him to explore various avenues and tap into multiple sources of income. As time progressed, he continued to nurture and expand these streams, recognising that the more diverse the revenue sources, the greater the financial resilience and potential for further success. With each new addition, the entrepreneurial journey grows richer and more rewarding, propelling us further down the road of a wealthy mindset.

Examples of Multiple Revenue Streams: In the world of financial abundance, multiple revenue streams are essential for prosperity. Gone are the days when a single source of income could dictate our destinies. In this most dynamic era for humanity, we must continue to learn to embrace the multiple possibilities that lie within our grasp. So, let's explore the diverse avenues that lead to the destination of wealth:

1. **Salary & Bonus**: A long-time dependable pillar of financial stability, salaries and bonuses offer a regular inflow of funds in exchange for our time, dedicated efforts, and expertise. It serves as the foundation upon which we can build our financial endeavours as an employee.

2. **Day Rate**: For the confident, creative, and skilled in their chosen field, the day rate unveils a world of opportunity. It allows us to lend our time, talents, and services to clients on a daily basis as a contractor, offering flexibility and the potential for lucrative compensation and, more importantly, flexibility.

3. **Retainers**: Another realm of consultancy available to those who wield specialised knowledge. Retainers ensure a promise of ongoing collaboration, where we serve as trusted advisors, offering insights and guidance to clients who value our expertise, continuing the flexibility that is built into the consultancy alternative. Both day rates and retainers require you to be able to sell your products and services as a consultant, and as you grow a business, those of others too.

4. **Dividends**: Within the realm of investments, dividends emerge as a testament to our foresight, decisiveness, and discernment. They represent a share in the profits earned by companies we have invested in as a shareholder or owner, providing a steady stream of income that rewards our financial acumen.

5. **Royalties**: For the creatives and innovators, royalties hold the promise of reaping the rewards of our intellectual pursuits. Whether through books, music, or other artistic endeavours, royalties grant us the opportunity to profit from the fruits of our creative efforts.

6. **Investments**: The art of investing, a dance with risk and reward, offers some wonderful possibilities. From stocks to real estate, bonds to cryptocurrencies, investments serve as fertile ground for nurturing our wealth, harnessing the power of compounding returns and market appreciation. Compounding is a great part of your investment strategy. Compounding is a financial phenomenon that makes time work in your favour. It's what happens when your investment earnings are added to your principal, forming a larger base on which earnings may accumulate. And as your investment base gets larger, it has the potential to grow faster. Over 45% of Paul's net worth is compounding, with investments long term in cash, equities, and bonds.

7. **Appreciation**: As the world evolves and the tides of fortune ebb and flow, our assets can bear witness to appreciation. Whether it be real estate properties, owned companies, artwork, metals, or other collectibles, their

value can grow over time, giving us the gift of increased wealth as the years roll by.

It is important to make your decisions on your preferred route of income and lifestyle, while remaining flexible as needed. Decisions are habits. Deciding and committing to a decision is a powerful message to the universe that you are ready and willing to do what it takes to reach your chosen destination.

Moving further beyond the array of revenue streams at our disposal, it is essential to delve deeper into their payment schemes. Understanding how these revenues flow into our lives unlocks another realm of possibilities, enabling us to harness their potential for diverse opportunities and navigate the intricacies of taxation. Let us embark on this exploration of financial intricacies:

1. **Meeting Basic Needs**: Our primary consideration lies in utilising these revenues to meet our fundamental necessities. From food, clothing, and shelter to education and healthcare, ensuring that our basic needs are fulfilled forms the bedrock of both mental and financial stability. By allocating the appropriate portion of our earnings towards these essentials, we establish a solid foundation upon which to build our future endeavours.

2. **Roll-Over Investments**: The allure of growth and expansion beckons, and our revenue streams can serve as a roll-over opportunity. By rolling over a portion of our earnings for further investment, we sow the seeds of additional financial prosperity.

3. **Generating Cash for New Opportunities**: Entrepreneurial spirits are fuelled by the desire to seize new opportunities as they arise. Our revenue streams can be harnessed to generate the cash necessary to pursue these fresh prospects. Whether it be launching a new business, venturing into a different industry, or acquiring assets that hold great potential, having readily available cash from our revenues opens doors to exciting new opportunities and horizons.

4. **Generating Cash for Guilt and Worry-Free Spending**: Amidst the pursuit of financial abundance, it is crucial to carve out space for guilt-free spending. Our revenue streams hold the power to not only meet our basic needs and fuel further investments but also to grant us the freedom to enjoy the fruits of our labour without concern or worry.

5. **Tax Considerations:** As we traverse the landscape of financial prosperity, we must understand and navigate the realm of taxes. Each revenue stream carries with it certain tax implications that need careful consideration. By understanding the intricacies of tax regulations and seeking the guidance of professionals, we can ensure that our earnings are managed in a responsible and compliant manner. By staying informed and taking advantage of applicable tax strategies, we can optimise our financial position and mitigate undue burdens.

By comprehending the payment schemes of our revenue streams, we unlock the keys to a world of opportunities. Let's consider some of Paul's revenue streams and how payment schemes influence these:

- Company #1 monthly retainer*.
- Company #2 monthly retainer*.
- Company #1 annual dividends (passive)*.
- Company #2 annual dividends (passive)*.
- Company #1 appreciation (passive) – recognised when you sell**.
- Company #2 appreciation (passive) – recognised when you sell**.
- Gold appreciation (passive) – recognised when you sell**.
- Silver appreciation (passive) – recognised when you sell**.
- Property appreciation (passive) – recognised when you sell**.
- Property monthly rentals (passive)*.
- Investment portfolio appreciation (passive) – reinvested each month**.
- Crypto appreciation (passive) – reinvested each month**.
- Whisky appreciation (passive) – recognised when you sell**.
- Watches appreciation (passive) – recognised when you sell**.
- Book monthly sales or associated opportunities (passive)*.

*Short-term cash generators – less than 1 year.

**Long-term wealth generators – when you sell.

These are just some of the diverse streams that converge to form a river of money, wealth, and prosperity. In this age of endless opportunities, we can all choose to embrace the wisdom of diversification, understanding that a multitude of revenue streams holds the key to financial resilience, independence, and the fulfilment of our dreams. We both appreciate that these multiple sources of income take time to create—they have for both of us—but this is your life and your lifetime. Choose how you spend your time and money wisely. Learn from the best; often, the most effective way to achieve is to be coached by someone who is already living the way you'd like to live.

Part 13 - Assets & Liabilities: Understanding the Distinction Between Wealth Building and Debt

Defining an asset or liability can often cause confusion, so let's consider the following definition from a cash flow perspective:

It's an asset if it makes you money and a liability if it costs you money.

You could also consider the people around you in this manner: are they assets to your journey, or are they liabilities?

If you think about it from a cash flow perspective, the house you live in—or do not rent out—and the car you drive are liabilities. Unless they appreciate in value and you sell them, they will continue to be liabilities.

Do not always think about an asset as something that is worth money when you sell it; you also need to factor in what that asset costs you today and how this will influence your cash flow.

Part 14 - Tracking Your Financial Wealth: Implementing Systems to Monitor and Evaluate Financial Progress

Tracking your financial wealth is an essential practice for managing your personal finances effectively. It involves monitoring and evaluating your assets, liabilities, income, and expenses to gain a clear understanding of your financial health and make informed decisions about your money. By keeping a close eye on your wealth, you can make informed decisions, set realistic GOALS, and take appropriate actions to improve your financial health.

Here are a few key points to consider when tracking your financial wealth:

1. **Short-Term Cash & Expenses**: Start by writing down your income sources and categorising your expenses. Tracking your expenses allows you to identify areas where you can cut back and save more money. A wealthy mindset involves the concept of circulating money. However, control and prioritise your own expenses, always pay yourself first, and do not use the purpose of "circulating the money" as an excuse for overspending. Any individual who consistently overspends may well have an issue that needs to be looked at in coaching, or possibly therapy, to improve their self-image and beliefs around money.

2. **Net Worth Calculation**: Calculate your net worth regularly by subtracting your liabilities (such as loans, mortgages, and credit card debt) from your assets (including cash, investments, real estate, and other valuables). Tracking your net worth over time helps you gauge your financial progress. Wealthy financial people think about net worth as opposed to net income.

3. **Financial Statements**: Maintain updated financial statements, including bank statements, investment account statements, and credit card statements. These statements provide a clear overview of your financial transactions, helping you identify any discrepancies and track your spending patterns.

4. **Investment Tracking**: If you have investments in stocks, bonds, mutual funds, or other financial instruments, regularly review their performance. Track your investment returns, and assess whether they align with your financial GOALS and risk tolerance.

5. **Retirement Planning**: For those who want to retire, monitor your retirement savings, and track the growth of your retirement accounts. Project your future retirement needs, and adjust as necessary to ensure you're on track for a comfortable retirement. Retirement planning is an interesting area because Mark & Paul no longer think about retirement and Paul has cashed in his pensions. When you look at their GOALS, they both wanted to become independent from any government help and fend for themselves, which they achieved several years ago. When you look at the government pensions now available in the UK, that was certainly one of Paul's best decisions in life. They no longer need to rely on the UK government to provide them with pension money, which means they are truly financially independent. Bob Proctor used to say, "Create your own economy," and we have both been on our own journeys towards this GOAL for some time. Pensions can be a complicated area, so it's better to seek financial

advice on how you work through such issues. There are many good pensions out there, so we would not recommend this approach taken by Mark and Paul as a fit-for-all way forward. However, it worked for both.

6. **Debt Management**: Keep track of your debts, including outstanding balances, interest rates, and repayment schedules. Tracking your debt allows you to prioritise repayment and develop strategies to reduce or eliminate it. Debt (and especially bad debt) is one of the most mismanaged parts of financial wealth and the most feared by many, where the public narrative encourages the use of credit cards and loans. However, the outcome is that many individuals and families are in debt that they cannot see a way to dig themselves out of. Our advice is simply to throw out the shovel and make debt management one of your priority GOALS to reduce it.

Mark commented that many people have the GOAL to get out of debt. The truth is that way of thinking will keep you in debt forever. Whether we're thinking "get in" or "get out," if we're thinking of debt, we'll attract more debt. Set up an automated repayment program, and start to think about prosperity. Many successful millionaires and multimillionaires that are household names have used creative debt in managing their finances successfully and then leveraged responsibly from lenders.

Paul commented that he is one of those multimillionaires within the top UK 0.15% of wealth generators and sees debt as the major obstacle to those who want to be a millionaire, and he is not the exception to this debt-free approach. Many people have tried to use debt, and many have failed. Many individuals are greedy and see using debt as the quick and easy solution. However, when conditions change, this approach can cause the house of cards to come tumbling down. The housing crisis, recent interest rate increases, and COVID were all disastrous for many individuals when they over-leveraged.

A few years ago, a friend asked Mark for some advice on how he could manage his debt situation. The starting point was to cut up those credit cards because he was not in a position mentally or materially to continue incurring increasing debts. Then he started on an automated pay-down plan so he could get out of this hole, and through coaching, he learned to focus on prosperity.

7. **Financial SMART GOALS**: Set specific financial GOALS, such as saving for a down payment on property, paying off a student loan, paying off credit card debts, or building an emergency fund. Regularly track your progress towards these GOALS and adjust as needed to stay on course. The COVID years were a difficult time for many who did not have that emergency fund. That's a lesson we should all keep in mind and build into our financial GOALS. We recommend you also read or listen to *Life Remixed* (and again and again until your subconscious has internalised the messages within its pages), as it contains Mark's recovery from

his own financial meltdown during the financial crisis of 2008/9.

8. **Utilise Technology**: Take advantage of personal finance software or mobile apps that can automate the tracking process. These tools can help you categorise expenses, generate reports, and provide visual representations of your financial data. Also, be aware that you can sometimes use such tools and over-analyse the tracking. Sometimes it's wise to start simply and build from there.

Remember, tracking your financial wealth is not just about numbers; it is about your thoughts, feelings, and actions aligning so that your beliefs around money are positive. Then it's about gaining control over your finances and making better, more informed decisions. Regularly reviewing and analysing your financial situation allows you to identify areas for improvement, make necessary adjustments, and work towards achieving long-term financial stability and success.

One of the fundamental aspects of tracking your financial wealth is creating a comprehensive list of your expenses that are prioritised. A prioritised list of expenses helps you allocate your income to various categories, such as housing, transportation, food, entertainment, and savings. By tracking your expenses and prioritising, you can identify areas where you may be overspending and make necessary adjustments to achieve your financial GOALS.

In addition to expenses, it is crucial to keep track of your assets and liabilities. Your assets may include cash, investments, real estate, vehicles, and valuable possessions, while liabilities encompass debts like mortgages, student loans, credit card balances, and personal loans. Don't forget those payments for running your car and the house you live in. Maintaining an up-to-date record of these financial components allows you to assess your net worth accurately.

We use Excel spreadsheets to keep track of these items and review our finances two or three times each week (Paul) and twice a month (Mark).

Regularly reviewing and analysing your financial progress is another vital aspect of tracking your wealth. By periodically assessing your income, expenses, savings, and investments, you can identify trends, evaluate your financial decisions, and adjust your GOALS and strategies accordingly. It helps you stay on top of your financial GOALS and make informed choices about spending, saving, and investing.

Part 15 - Assess Your Current Status: Taking Stock of One's Financial Standing and Trajectory

Some questions to ask yourself:

- Do you know what your current net worth is?
- What debt do you owe?
- Do you keep track of your financial wealth?
- Do you know how much you make each month?
- Is this broken down into revenue streams?
- Do you know what your monthly expenses are?
- Do you prioritise your monthly expenses?
- How much free cash are you generating each month?

- Do you track what your assets are?
- Do you track your liabilities?
- What amount do you have as an emergency fund?
- Do you have financial wealth-related GOALS?
- How are you learning and developing your business skills?
- Are you applying any knowledge gained, including your business skills?

Part 16 - Tax Planning: Strategies for Minimising Tax Burdens and Maximising Efficiency

There are two certainties in life: death and taxes.

Tax planning refers to the process of organising your financial affairs in a way that minimises your tax liability within the legal framework. It involves making strategic decisions and taking advantage of various tax incentives, deductions, and exemptions provided by the tax laws.

Here are some common strategies used in tax planning:

1. **Understanding Tax Laws**: Stay informed about the tax laws relevant to your jurisdiction, including any recent changes. This knowledge will help you identify opportunities for minimising taxes.

2. **Income Splitting**: If you have family members in a lower tax bracket, you can legally allocate income to them to reduce the overall tax burden. This strategy is often used by business owners or high-income individuals.

3. **Maximise Deductions and Credits**: Take advantage of all eligible deductions and tax credits available to

you. This may include deductions for mortgage interest, medical expenses, charitable donations, education expenses, or retirement contributions.

4. **Retirement Planning Where Necessary**: Contribute to tax-advantaged retirement accounts. These contributions are often tax-deductible, and the investment growth is tax-deferred until withdrawal, depending on where you are a resident.

5. **Capital Gains and Losses**: Consider the tax implications of selling investments. By strategically timing the sale of assets with capital gains or losses, you can manage your taxable income.

6. **Tax-Efficient Investments**: Use investments that provide tax advantages.

7. **Business Structure**: For business owners, choosing the right business entity (e.g., sole trader, sole proprietorship, partnership, corporation, etc.), and place of registration, can have significant tax implications. Consulting with a tax professional can help determine the most tax-efficient structure for your business. We have trusted tax professionals available to us globally and have received the best advice for each jurisdiction we operate in.

8. **Estate Planning**: Develop an estate plan that minimises estate and inheritance taxes. This may involve setting up trusts, gifting assets during your lifetime, or utilising other estate planning strategies depending on where you are a resident, non-resident, and non-domiciled perhaps, which passport you hold, and the tax laws that apply.

In the complex world of taxation, there are three distinct paths: tax optimisation, tax avoidance, and tax evasion. Each path carries its own implications and consequences. Tax optimisation is the realm of the proactive, where meticulous planning and analysis take place long before taxes are due. It involves employing legitimate strategies to structure finances in a way that minimises the tax burden. On the other hand, tax avoidance comes into play after taxes have arisen. It involves leveraging the intricacies of tax laws to ethically reduce the amount owed through deductions and other legal means. Tax avoidance is a strategic dance within the boundaries of the law. However, it is vital not to confuse avoidance with tax evasion—a dark path characterised by deception and fraudulent actions. Tax evasion is a deliberate attempt to evade taxes by concealing income, misrepresenting financial transactions, or engaging in illegal activities. It is a treacherous road that leads to severe penalties and legal consequences. In the pursuit of peace of mind, a wealthy mindset, and financial harmony, understanding these divergent paths is essential to navigating the intricate system of taxation with integrity and foresight.

In the ever-evolving landscape of taxation, an array of factors comes into play when considering your tax obligations. It begins with the recognition that your passport can have implications on the taxes you owe. Different countries employ diverse taxation systems, and your citizenship can determine the extent of your tax liability. Residency, too, holds great significance. The place you call home, where you establish your primary residence, can establish the foundation for your tax obligations. Beyond that, the nature of your income becomes a crucial consideration. Whether you earn through day rates, retainers, dividends, or other means, the classification of your income can shape the tax treatments it receives. Furthermore, the location where your income is paid assumes importance. Different jurisdictions may have varying tax regulations on income earned within their borders or income received from foreign sources. Grappling with these complex factors demands a careful understanding of the tax laws applicable to your situation. Seeking professional advice from trusted tax experts or consulting relevant resources becomes indispensable in ensuring compliance and making informed decisions to optimise your tax position.

To embark on a journey of tax optimisation, the first step is to understand the tax laws that apply to your specific circumstances. It is crucial to familiarise yourself with the tax regulations of your home country, as well as any potential international tax implications. By being proactive and gaining knowledge about tax laws, you can identify opportunities and strategies for optimising your tax position.

Another avenue to explore is the possibility of changing your place of residency. This decision can have a profound impact on your tax obligations and financial wealth. By relocating to a jurisdiction with more favourable tax laws, you may be able to maximise your tax optimisation efforts. However, it is crucial to approach this with careful consideration and thorough planning. Changing residency involves various legal and practical considerations, and maintaining compliance with both your current and new tax jurisdictions is paramount.

In examining the scenario of an individual in the United Kingdom who falls within the top 1% of earners as of March

2023, we can draw a compelling comparison to someone who has strategically addressed tax optimisation matters, thereby avoiding tax obligations altogether. The potential benefits that can be reaped from such a course of action are undeniably significant. By changing their tax burdens, this individual effectively propels themselves into a higher echelon, positioning themselves towards the top 0.5% of earners in the UK. The disparity in financial standing between these two example individuals serves as a testament to the substantial advantages that can be gained by adeptly navigating the complex world of tax optimisation.

UK Earnings top 1% (May 2023)			UK Non-Resident		
			Cash Earnings (tax free)	Dividend Cash (tax free)	
Gross earnings to be in UK top 1%		£ 201,048.00	£ 113,681.00	£ 65,000.00	Combined amount GBP 178,681 - 13% less
Tax					
Up to GBP 12,570	0%	£ -	£ -	£ -	
GBP 12,571 to GBP 50,270	20%	£ 7,540.00	£ -	£ -	
GBP 50,271 to GBP 125,140	40%	£ 29,947.60	£ -	£ -	
Over GBP 125,140	45%	£ 34,158.60	£ -	£ -	
Income tax due		£ 71,646.20	£ -	£ -	
Earnings after income tax		£ 129,401.80	£ 113,681.00	£ 65,000.00	
National Insurance					
Up to GBP 1,256 per year.	0%	£ -	£ -	£ -	
GBP 1,256.01 to GBP 50,268 per year.	12%	£ 5,881.44	£ -	£ -	
Over GBP 50,268 per year.	2%	£ 3,015.60	£ -	£ -	
Total NI		£ 8,897.04	£ -	£ -	
Net earnings		£ 120,504.76	£ 178,681.00		48% better off

Figure 2 – The Impact of Tax

Reflecting on personal experiences, Paul's decision to become a UK non-resident over two decades ago proved to be one of his most astute financial moves. By adhering to the overseas compliance tests, he successfully optimised his tax position and reaped the benefits. This serves as a reminder that making informed decisions and staying up to date with tax regulations can have a lasting impact on your financial success.

In the pursuit of tax optimisation, it is essential to exercise caution and consult trusted tax professionals who can provide guidance tailored to your unique circumstances. By understanding the relevant tax laws, exploring residency options, and learning from others' real-life examples, you can set yourself on a path towards maximising your financial potential through effective tax strategies.

Part 17 - Managing & Protecting Wealth: Safeguarding Assets and Mitigating Risks

Achieving financial prosperity requires not only building wealth but also protecting it. Creating financial wealth and managing or safeguarding it are distinct challenges. The following areas are crucial to consider:

1. **Estate Planning**: Effective estate planning is fundamental to successful wealth management, offering individuals a comprehensive toolkit to optimise their assets and ensure their distribution aligns with their desired outcomes. Through the strategic use of wills, trusts, and a deep understanding of inheritance tax laws, individuals can safeguard their wealth, minimise tax liabilities, and ensure a smooth and efficient transfer of assets to their chosen beneficiaries. For example, in the UK, any net worth over GBP 325,000 is potentially taxed at 40%, meaning a significant portion of your estate could end up with the government rather than

with your loved ones. It is, therefore, crucial to seek the right advice to manage such situations effectively.

2. **Wills**: A cornerstone of estate planning, wills play a vital role in protecting and distributing wealth according to an individual's wishes after their passing. A will serves as a legal document that outlines how assets, properties, and possessions should be distributed among beneficiaries. It provides clarity and guidance, ensuring that loved ones are taken care of and assets are managed in line with your intentions. Seeking professional help is advisable, as multiple wills may be required depending on the location of your assets. For example, Paul had to create and update four separate wills to cover his various assets in different countries.

3. **Country-Specific Assets**: When you have assets in multiple countries, it's important to consider the concept of "domicile" or "residency" as it relates to estate planning. Your domicile or primary residence typically governs the distribution of your overall estate. However, for assets located in other countries, the laws of those jurisdictions may also apply.

4. **Inheritance Tax**: Also known as estate tax or death tax in some jurisdictions, inheritance tax is imposed on the transfer of assets from a deceased individual to their beneficiaries. It is a form of taxation that occurs at the time of inheritance or bequest and is based on the total value of the assets being passed down. Some countries impose inheritance tax while others do not, so it's crucial to be aware of the laws that apply to you.

5. **Inheritance Tax Specifics**: Rates, exemptions, and thresholds vary from country to country. Some countries have a progressive tax system, where the tax rate increases with the value of the inherited assets, while others have a fixed tax rate regardless of the asset value.

6. **Purpose of Inheritance Tax**: Inheritance tax generates revenue for the government and redistributes wealth within society. It is often levied on assets such as real estate, investments, cash, and valuable personal belongings. However, certain assets, such as those passing to a surviving spouse or charitable organisations, may be exempt from inheritance tax.

7. **Mitigating the Impact of Inheritance Tax**: Many individuals engage in estate planning strategies to minimise the impact of inheritance tax. These strategies may involve creating trusts, gifting assets during their lifetime, or utilising exemptions and deductions available under the tax laws. Proper estate planning can help reduce overall tax liability, allowing individuals to pass on their wealth to their intended beneficiaries more efficiently. It's important to note that inheritance tax laws are subject to change, so consulting with a knowledgeable and trusted tax advisor or estate planning attorney is crucial to understanding the specific rules and regulations in your jurisdiction. By proactively considering inheritance tax in your estate planning efforts, you can better protect your assets and ensure a smooth transfer of wealth to your loved ones.

8. **Trusts**: Trusts are powerful legal structures that play a significant role in protecting and managing wealth. A

trust is created when a person (the "grantor" or "settlor") transfers assets to a separate legal entity (the "trust") to be held and managed by a designated individual or entity (the "trustee") for the benefit of one or more beneficiaries. Trusts offer a range of benefits and serve various purposes in wealth protection.

9. **Trust Benefits**: One primary advantage of trusts is their ability to provide asset protection. By placing assets in a trust, they are held separately from personal ownership, reducing the risk of creditors or legal claims accessing those assets. This is particularly valuable for individuals seeking to shield their wealth from potential lawsuits, business risks, or other liabilities. Trusts also offer control and flexibility over the distribution of assets. The grantor can define specific instructions on how and when assets should be distributed to beneficiaries, allowing for customised estate planning that protects assets for future generations and considers unique family circumstances.

10. **Trusts & Estate Planning**: In addition to asset protection and distribution control, trusts can help minimise estate taxes and probate costs. Depending on the type of trust established and the jurisdiction's laws, assets held in a trust may receive favourable tax treatment or even be exempt from taxes. Moreover, trusts can bypass the probate process, which can be time-consuming, costly, and subject to public scrutiny.

11. **Types of Trusts**: Common types of trusts include revocable living trusts, irrevocable trusts, charitable trusts, and special needs trusts. Each type has specific

purposes and benefits, tailored to address different objectives of wealth protection and distribution.

12. **Establishing a Trust**: Establishing a trust requires careful planning and consideration of legal and financial aspects. Consulting with an experienced estate planning solicitor or trust specialist is crucial to determine the most suitable trust structure for your specific GOALS and to ensure compliance with relevant laws and regulations.

13. **Financial Portfolio Allocation**: In today's fast-paced and ever-changing world, financial stability is a paramount concern for those seeking a secure future. Enter the balanced financial portfolio, a comprehensive approach that brings harmony and stability to one's financial pursuits. From stocks and bonds to real estate and commodities, each piece of the puzzle needs to be carefully examined, based on the level of risk you are willing to take. Often, your risk profile will determine whether you prefer a conservative, balanced, or growth-oriented portfolio.

The specific percentages for a balanced financial portfolio can vary depending on individual circumstances, GOALS, and risk tolerance. However, as a general guideline, a balanced portfolio typically aims to distribute investments across different asset classes in the following approximate proportions:

- **Stocks**: Around 40% to 60% of the portfolio may be allocated to stocks or equity-based investments. This category offers the potential for higher returns but also carries a higher level of risk.

- **Bonds**: Approximately 20% to 50% of the portfolio may be allocated to bonds or fixed-income investments. Bonds provide more stability and income generation compared to stocks, making them a valuable component for balancing risk.

- **Cash and Cash Equivalents**: Roughly 5% to 20% of the portfolio may be held in cash or cash equivalents such as money market funds or short-term Treasury bills. This allocation provides liquidity and serves as a cushion for emergencies or short-term needs.

- **Real Estate and Alternative Investments**: Approximately 10% to 50% of the portfolio may be allocated to real estate, commodities, or alternative investments. These assets offer diversification and can act as a hedge against inflation or provide exposure to unique opportunities.

It's important to note that these percentages are not fixed and can be adjusted based on individual preferences, market conditions, and investment strategies. Consulting with a financial advisor is always recommended to tailor a balanced financial portfolio to your specific circumstances and GOALS.

Why Invest in Gold and Silver?

Investing in gold and silver is a way of storing financial wealth. With around USD 121 to USD 197 billion traded each day, these metals are scarce enough to remain precious due to their utility. Central banks continue to buy gold, which can hold its value over time and offset market volatility in stocks, bonds, and property. However, some consider gold an "unproductive asset." Currently priced at over USD 2,500 per ounce, gold has risen by approximately 30% in the past year, 73% in the last five years, 92% over the last decade, and 525% over the last 20 years. Here's why Paul has invested a small portion of his portfolio in gold and silver:

1. **Hedge Against Inflation**: Gold and silver have historically served as hedges against inflation. When fiat currency values decrease due to rising inflation, the price of gold and silver tends to rise, preserving purchasing power and providing a store of value.

2. **Diversification**: Including gold and silver in a portfolio helps diversify risk. These precious metals have different market dynamics compared to stocks and bonds, meaning they can perform differently under various economic conditions. Their inclusion can reduce overall portfolio volatility and offer a potential counterbalance to other investments.

3. **Safe Haven Assets**: During times of economic uncertainty, gold and silver often act as safe haven assets. Investors flock to them as a perceived safe store of value when traditional markets experience turbulence, geopolitical tensions rise, or confidence in the financial system wanes.

4. **Tangible Assets**: Unlike stocks or bonds, gold and silver are tangible assets. They hold intrinsic value and can be physically owned, providing a sense of security and protection against systemic risks associated with paper-based investments.

5. **Portfolio Insurance**: Gold and silver can serve as a form of insurance within a portfolio. If other investments, such as stocks or currencies, suffer significant downturns, the value of gold and silver may rise, offsetting losses and helping to protect overall portfolio value.

However, it's important to remember that gold and silver come with their own risks, such as price volatility and limited income generation. As with any investment, it's advisable to carefully evaluate your financial GOALS and risk tolerance, and consult with a financial advisor before deciding to include gold and silver in your portfolio.

Stock Picking: A Cautionary Tale

Stock picking is a challenging endeavour—everyone fancies themselves an expert. Berkshire Hathaway invests in around 48 stocks, but 85% of its value lies in just eight companies:

- Apple (AAPL)
- Bank of America (BAC)
- American Express Co. (AXP)
- Coca-Cola Co. (KO)
- Chevron (CVX)
- Occidental Petroleum (OXY)
- Kraft Heinz (KHC)
- Moody's Corp. (MCO)

Paul uses investment management companies to handle most of his equities, bonds, and alternative investments through a trust vehicle that accounts for approximately 38% of his net worth. You pay a fee, but you receive sound advice in return.

You might want to scratch that itch of picking some equities yourself, but don't bet the farm on it. Paul has USD 34,000 in personally picked equities (0.3% of his net worth) to this pursuit, hoping it will continue to compound. He uses 50% ETFs along with a few selected stocks, which he leaves long-term to compound:

- Apple (AAPL)
- Amazon (AMZN)
- American Express Co. (AXP)
- Berkshire Hathaway B (BRK.B)
- Coca-Cola Co. (KO)
- Meta Platforms (META)
- Microsoft (MSFC)
- NVIDIA Corp. (NVDA)
- Procter & Gamble (PG)
- Schwab Dividend (SCHD)
- Shopify (SHOP)
- INVESCO NASDAQ 100 ETF (QQQM)
- Schwab International Equity ETF (SCHF)
- Vanguard S&P 500 ETF (VOO)
- Vanguard Information Technology ETF (VGT)

Cryptocurrency: A Gamble Worth Taking?

Cryptocurrency is another challenging path—one of those itches you might want to scratch. Paul allocated USD 30,000 to Bitcoin and Ethereum, now worth over USD 100,000 (0.8% of his net worth). This gain is mostly down to luck, and Paul intends to leave it to compound further.

Paul's Current Portfolio Breakdown:

- Trust (equities, bonds, alternatives, & cash): 38%

- Real Estate: 28%
- Commodities (bullion - gold and silver): 13%
- Cash: 8%
- Company Ownership (valued as break-up amount, no goodwill): 7%
- Miscellaneous: 6% (crypto, personal shares, whiskey, watches, cars, and miscellaneous investments)

Mark, on the other hand, holds interests in ten UK companies and various other partnerships. He has been dubbed a serial entrepreneur since his personal challenges documented in *Life Remixed*. His main focus is UK property, writing books that help others, public speaking, success coaching, and growing each of these companies through worldwide sales of goods and services.

Together, portfolio allocations, wills, trusts, and a thorough understanding of inheritance tax laws create a powerful framework for individuals to manage, protect, and distribute their wealth in a manner that reflects their values and aspirations. By consulting with experienced professionals and implementing a well-crafted estate plan, individuals can achieve their desired outcomes, provide for their loved ones, and leave a lasting legacy beyond mere financial assets.

Despite being a multimillionaire, Paul continues to invest in himself with his order of priorities being needs/investing/wants, focusing on his net worth as a wealthy individual, comparing this to rich and poor people, who focus on their net income, where their priorities are wants/needs/investing, the outcome is quite considerable.

As a rule:

- Surround yourself with positive people when considering financial wealth building and protection.

- Avoid spending time with negative people, especially when working on financial wealth building and protection.

Then, consider the following questions:

- Have you considered how to balance your portfolio?
- Do you have the wills you need?
- Have you considered seeking advice on estate planning?
- Have you considered using trusts?

Part 18 - Financial Experts: Leveraging Professional Advice and Expertise

Financial experts, often referred to as financial advisors or planners, play a crucial role in helping individuals and businesses navigate the complex world of finance and make informed decisions. These professionals possess a deep understanding of various financial concepts, products, and strategies, and they provide personalised guidance based on their clients' specific needs and GOALS.

One of the primary responsibilities of financial experts is to assess their clients' financial situations and develop comprehensive plans tailored to their unique circumstances. They evaluate factors such as income, expenses, assets, and liabilities to create strategies for budgeting, saving, investing, and debt management. By analysing these components, financial experts can offer recommendations that optimise their clients' financial wealth and support their long-term objectives.

Investment planning is another essential area where financial experts excel. They assess clients' risk tolerance, time horizon, and financial GOALS to develop investment portfolios that align with their objectives. Financial experts stay informed about market trends, economic conditions, and investment opportunities to provide informed advice on asset allocation, diversification, and investment selection. Their expertise helps clients maximise returns while managing risks within their investment portfolios.

Ultimately, financial experts serve as trusted partners who empower individuals and businesses to make sound financial decisions. They offer objective advice, monitor progress, and adjust strategies as needed to keep their clients on track towards their financial GOALS. By leveraging their expertise, individuals and businesses can navigate financial complexities with confidence and achieve greater financial security and success.

In the vast and complex realm of finance, Mark and Paul have both spent considerable time seeking the perfect financial expert advice. However, this pursuit has proved challenging, as the financial landscape is riddled with unregulated providers and dubious characters. It took Paul a staggering 12 years to find someone with whom he felt comfortable and who possessed the necessary knowledge and integrity to guide him through the labyrinthine paths of wealth management. For Mark, tapping into a network through working with a UK wealth coach started the journey towards improving his financial wealth. However, even now, as they work with these chosen advisors, they remain vigilant and unrelenting in scrutinising their consistency and performance. The world of finance demands a delicate balance of caution and curiosity, where one must tread carefully, mindful of the risks lurking beneath the shimmering and shiny surface.

In the intricate tapestry of their financial journeys, Mark and Paul have adopted a discerning approach when seeking advice for preserving and growing their wealth. Paul's net worth is approaching the top 0.15% and Mark's within the top 5% to 10% of the UK.

After his bankruptcy 15 years ago, Mark has made remarkable strides in rebuilding his financial wealth, climbing into the upper ranks of the UK's wealth distribution. 'While I may not be among the ultra-wealthy (yet), reaching the top 5% to 10% of the population is a significant achievement. It brings a sense of financial security but also highlights the stark contrast between those at different points on the financial spectrum. Moving from bankruptcy to this level has deepened my understanding of these disparities,' he reflects. 'Many view this as a mark of success, but for me, it carries a greater responsibility. It's a chance to share the insights that come with a wealthy mindset approach, and that's what *Money Remixed* is all about—passing on these learnings.'

Both Mark and Paul are acutely aware of the importance of only seeking guidance from individuals whose expertise and success align with their own aspirations. Consequently, they exercise caution and prudence, choosing not to entrust the delicate intricacies of their financial empire to those whose net worth or earnings fall significantly short of their own. In pursuing sound financial counsel, they recognise the value of seeking advice from those who have traversed similar paths of success and accomplishment, as their insights and experiences are more likely to resonate with their continued aspirations.

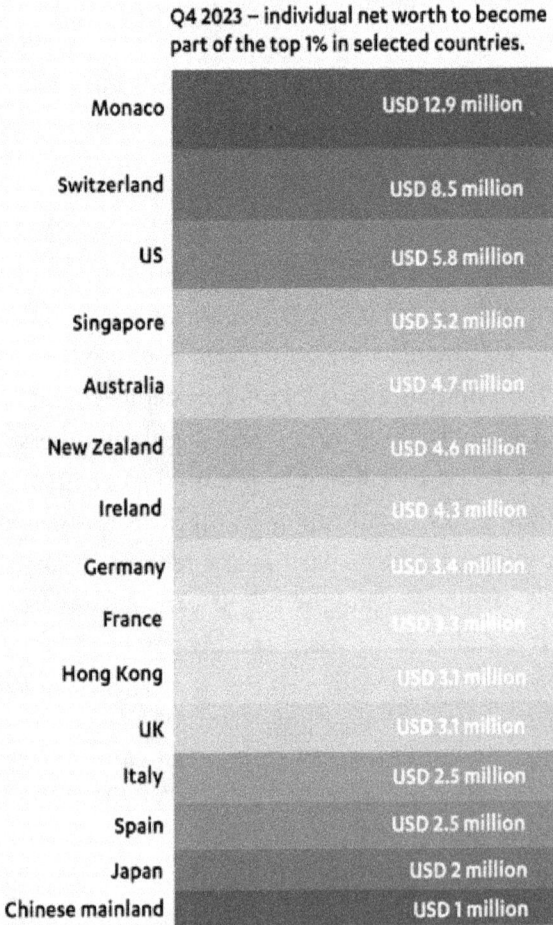

Q4 2023 – individual net worth to become part of the top 1% in selected countries.

Monaco	USD 12.9 million
Switzerland	USD 8.5 million
US	USD 5.8 million
Singapore	USD 5.2 million
Australia	USD 4.7 million
New Zealand	USD 4.6 million
Ireland	USD 4.3 million
Germany	USD 3.4 million
France	USD 3.3 million
Hong Kong	USD 3.1 million
UK	USD 3.1 million
Italy	USD 2.5 million
Spain	USD 2.5 million
Japan	USD 2 million
Chinese mainland	USD 1 million

Source: www research.

Figure 3 – Top 1% Q4 2023

Something else worth considering, when you start to delve into wealth building, maintaining wealth and looking for financial advice, where you live makes a difference: The cost of living in Thailand is around 20-40% lower than in Spain, 30-50% less than in Dubai, 40-60% lower than in the UK, 40-60% lower than in the USA, and 50-70% lower than in Singapore! Managing your expenses is very much part of wealth building and wealth maintaining. And it's hot all year round in Thailand.

Part 19 - Safeguarding Against Compliance Practitioners: Navigating Legal and Regulatory Frameworks Responsibly

Always seek the advice of experts on financial wealth building and protection—but be wary of compliance practitioners. It took Paul several years to find a trustworthy expert, and along the way, he encountered a few compliance practitioners who employed deceptive tactics, often preying on his wealth. These practitioners possess a keen understanding of human behaviour, exploiting automatic response patterns commonly known as the "click, whirr" response. By being aware of their tactics, you can effectively protect your wealth and make informed financial decisions. Some of the methods they use include:

1. **Material Self-Interest**: The illusion of a great deal often appeals to our desire for a bargain. Compliance practitioners leverage material self-interest, presenting themselves as offering an exceptional opportunity. However, it is crucial to critically evaluate such claims, ensuring they align with your long-term financial GOALS and considering potential hidden costs or risks.

2. **Reciprocation**: The give and take, and take again. Reciprocation is a powerful social norm that compliance practitioners exploit to create a sense of obligation. By providing a small favour or gift, they aim to elicit reciprocity, leading individuals to feel obliged to reciprocate by making a financial commitment. Vigilance is essential in recognising when genuine generosity ends and attempted manipulation begins.

3. **Commitment and Consistency**: People have a natural inclination to remain consistent with their past actions and decisions. Compliance practitioners capitalise on this tendency by seeking small commitments initially, making it easier to secure larger commitments later. Recognising this tactic can help you avoid being trapped in unwanted financial agreements.

4. **Social Proof**: The power of social proof lies in our tendency to rely on the actions and opinions of others when making decisions. Compliance practitioners employ this tactic by showcasing testimonials, positive reviews, or statistical data to create the impression that their offer is widely accepted. It is crucial to conduct independent research and seek diverse perspectives to make well-informed financial choices.

5. **Liking**: Compliance practitioners, the friendly thieves, understand the influence of likability on our decision-making. They strive to build rapport, charm, and trust, making it easier to manipulate our judgment. Recognising the distinction between genuine rapport and calculated manipulation can safeguard your wealth from these friendly thieves.

6. **Authority**: Compliance practitioners often leverage their perceived authority or association with trusted institutions to gain credibility and persuade individuals. It is essential to be discerning and not blindly trust their claims solely based on their authority. Verifying credentials and seeking multiple expert opinions can help you protect your wealth from deceptive practices.

7. **Scarcity**: The principle of scarcity is employed to create a sense of urgency and fear of missing out. Compliance practitioners often emphasise limited availability, exclusive offers, or time-limited deals to spur impulsive decisions. It is crucial to step back, assess the situation objectively, and evaluate whether the scarcity is real or manufactured to prevent hasty and regrettable financial choices.

By understanding these tactics and being mindful of your decision-making process, you can shield your wealth from compliance practitioners who seek to exploit your automatic behaviour patterns. Empower yourself with knowledge, critical thinking, and independent research to make informed financial decisions that align with your long-term GOALS.

Influence: The Psychology of Persuasion by Robert B. Cialdini discusses the tactics used by compliance practitioners, which can be employed both ethically and unethically. Be aware of these tactics.

Part 20 - Where Do I Start – Something to Consider: Practical Steps for Initiating the Journey Towards Financial Well-Being

The path to financial abundance is within your reach. By embracing lifelong learning, maximising your earning potential, and protecting your wealth, you set the stage for a prosperous future. Cultivating a learning and wealthy mindset is the starting point; stay resilient in the face of challenges, and take consistent action. Now is the time to embark on this transformative journey and unleash your full potential for financial abundance—it's all part of the *14 Steps to a Wealthy Mindset.*

A simple tip from Paul concerning your financial wealth: *Baby Steps Millionaire* by Dave Ramsey is one of the simpler ways to get yourself out of debt and into positive net-worth numbers. It makes a lot of sense and gets you started on the *14 Steps to a Wealthy Mindset.*

- Start with your emergency fund.
- Pay off all debt.
- Build your emergency fund—3 to 6 months of expenses.
- Invest at least 15% of your household income.
- Save for your children's education, and continue to invest in your own.
- Pay off your home early.
- Build wealth and give.

Give and Take, by Adam Grant, presents the fascinating secrets to givers' success, and adopting this approach can help set you up for success.

These and many other educational sources are listed in Chapter 8.

> *"I've been poor, and I am now wealthy, and I know which one I prefer."*
>
> – Mark Wilkinson

CHAPTER 6

⌒⌒⌒

14 STEPS TO A WEALTHY MINDSET

STEP 12 - MANAGING FEAR

*"I learned that courage was not the absence of fear,
but triumph over it. The brave man is not he who does
not feel afraid, but he who conquers that fear."*

– Nelson Mandela,
former President of South Africa

There are many books and ideas on how to overcome fear;
two that come to mind immediately are Susan Jeffers' *Feel
the Fear and Do It Anyway* and Napoleon Hill's *Think and
Grow Rich*, which includes a chapter titled "How to Outwit
the Six Ghosts of Fear." Both are on Mark's recommended
reading list, which you can find here:

www.markwilkinsonofficial.com/recommended-reading/

First, let's look at what fear really is. In the depths of every
human heart lies an ancient, primal instinct—a force that has
the power to both paralyse and propel us forward: fear. It is an

emotion we all grapple with from time to time, but how we manage and navigate through this vast ocean of fear ultimately defines our journey. In this book, we embark on a profound exploration into the intricacies of fear and unveil the secrets to mastering its grip.

Fear, in its various forms, can be a formidable force that holds us back from living a fulfilling and authentic life. Through Mark's Life Remixed™ Coaching, many have embarked on a transformative journey to explore and understand some of the most common fears that plague our existence. By unravelling the intricacies of these fears, we will uncover effective strategies for managing them and reclaiming our power to live with courage, purpose, and joy.

One major fear we can all potentially encounter at some point in our life is the fear of poverty. This fear can manifest as indifference towards opportunities, doubt in our abilities, constant worry about financial stability, excessive caution that hinders our progress, and a tendency to procrastinate when taking necessary actions. By examining the root causes of this fear and addressing the underlying beliefs and mindset patterns, we can develop a healthier relationship with money, cultivate an abundance consciousness, and take confident steps towards financial wealth.

In their pursuit of financial independence, both authors embarked on a journey that transcended the boundaries of fear and poverty. This GOAL served as a catalyst for breaking free from the limitations imposed by uncertainty and doubt. Along the way, Paul encountered a question that would test the very essence of his resolve: "What if you wake up tomorrow and everything is gone?" This was essentially the problem Mark faced in *Life Remixed*, one that eventually took away his fear of "losing it all."

To Paul's surprise, when faced with this question, it didn't elicit panic or distress. Instead, it ignited a fire of determination and resilience. Both authors have faced moments of loss and learned from such situations, and they have both succeeded. The knowledge and experience gained from those challenges became the foundation of their strength to rebuild.

With each setback, they grew wiser and ever more resourceful. No matter your age, you, too, can learn to adapt, persevere, and rebuild from the ground up. The prospect of starting anew no longer fills them with trepidation; instead, it energises them to go again, believing that they have the power to rise above any circumstance. In every crisis, there is an opportunity, and by choosing a resilient mindset and perceiving failure as a learning event, they choose to grow and enjoy the process. What's the difference between try and triumph? A little "umph!"

Another common fear is the fear of criticism. This fear often stems from a deep-seated need for approval and acceptance from others. It can manifest as a fear of being judged, ridiculed, or rejected, leading us to hold back our true selves and conform to societal expectations. By developing self-compassion, building resilience, and embracing our unique voice and perspective, we can navigate criticism with grace and confidence, staying true to our authentic selves. This often shows up as a fear of public speaking—but public speaking is the symptom, not the cause. However, like any fear, it can be overcome, largely by facing it and stepping miles outside of your comfort zone, as Mark did.

He once held a fear of public speaking (a fear of rejection), so he put on a *Life Remixed* book launch event with 150 people attending and stood on stage and spoke for eight hours! Fear faced, and now on to the next challenge. When you learn to love and accept yourself and understand that not everyone else will, you are truly free to think, feel, attract, and create only wonderful opportunities for yourself, always remembering that "what anyone else thinks is none of your business."

The fear of ill health is another fear that plagues many individuals. It encompasses the anxiety and worry surrounding physical well-being and the fear of suffering from chronic illnesses or debilitating conditions. By adopting a holistic approach to health, including physical exercise, healthy eating habits, stress management techniques, and cultivating a positive mindset, we can empower ourselves to take proactive steps towards wellness and build resilience to face health challenges with strength and determination.

In the captivating pages of *Life Remixed*, Mark takes us on a transformative journey, with Chapter 8 standing as a beacon of resilience and personal triumph. Within this chapter, Mark fearlessly delves into the depths of his health struggles, specifically his battle with an incurable dis-ease (Ankylosing Spondylitis or Axial Spa, as it is now known) and the ensuing knee operations and limiting physical abilities.

With remarkable candour and vulnerability, Mark recounts the physical pain and limitations that plagued his daily life. However, what sets this story apart is his realisation that the true source of his suffering lay not only in his knees or anywhere else in his body but in the disconnection between his mind, body, and spirit, and his thoughts, feelings, and actions.

Mark shares how he embarked on an inward exploration, seeking solace and healing from within. As he dug deep into his being, he discovered a profound truth: the key to overcoming his health challenges was to find inner peace and be at ease with himself.

Through diligent self-reflection and paying attention to how he fuelled his body, Mark developed a new perspective—one that embraced acceptance, gratitude, and self-compassion. By cultivating a state of being "at ease" within, he was able to release the "dis-ease" that had manifested physically in his body over many years.

The body reflects the mind, and Mark's story is a testament to the power of the mind-body connection and the remarkable ability of the human spirit to overcome adversity. As readers embark on this chapter, they are invited to witness a remarkable transformation and learn invaluable lessons on finding harmony, healing, and wholeness amidst life's challenges.

Life Remixed offers more than just a glimpse into one person's journey—it serves as a source of inspiration and empowerment for all who seek to redefine their own narratives, discover their inner strength, and ultimately live the life of a wealthy mindset. Mark Wilkinson's story is a beacon of hope, demonstrating how we can rewrite the script of our lives and emerge triumphant in the face of any obstacle. Thank you, Mark.

The fear of losing the love of someone we hold dear, or are emotionally attached to, can be a profound and heart-wrenching experience. This fear stems from our attachment to relationships and the fear of abandonment or rejection. It can also arise if you have given that person responsibility over your results and they are no longer around to help. By cultivating healthy communication, trust, and developing a sense of self-worth that is not solely dependent on another person or external validation, we can nurture deep and meaningful connections while also finding solace in our own inner strength and self-love. Once you practice self-love daily, it becomes a habit. Total acceptance of yourself and "what is" ensures much of this fear dissipates over time.

The fear of old age looms as a spectator in the corners of our minds, reminding us of our mortality and the passage of time. It encompasses the anxiety and apprehension surrounding the physical, mental, and emotional changes that come with aging. This fear often stems from a deep-rooted obsession with youth and an aversion to the natural progression of life. We can challenge these notions and embark on a journey to redefine our relationship with aging. As the saying goes, "The older I get, the wiser my decisions." A great quote to remember is, "Don't regret getting older; it is a privilege denied to many."

The fear of death, perhaps the most profound and universal fear, hovers over our existence like an impenetrable veil. It is a fear born from the recognition of our own mortality and the unknown realm that awaits us beyond the boundaries of life. However, by facing this fear head-on, we have the opportunity to cultivate a profound appreciation for life itself. We confront the fear of death by embracing the present moment fully. By practising mindfulness and living with a sense of gratitude and purpose, we can transcend the fear of the unknown future and find solace in the richness and gift of the present. The fear of death is also a strange thing to dwell on, as, unless someone comes up with an injection that means we can all live forever, it is going to happen to us all one day. Mark has decided that when he passes, it will be the way he has lived—with a smile on his face and nothing to fear as he moves on to the next part of his eternal journey. This way of thinking and feeling takes away any fear while we are living on this physical planet.

Fear has a cunning way of infiltrating the human mind, planting seeds of doubt and uncertainty through the persistent whispers of "what if." It paralyses humans, often being generational and pervading society, rendering us stagnant and immobile, trapped in a cycle of overthinking and indecision. To break free from its grip, we must first recognise this pattern and acknowledge its detrimental effects on our progress. Like a pause button halting our forward movement, fear prevents us from taking the necessary actions to reach our GOALS and fulfil our potential. It is only by mustering the courage to press our internal play button, to face and then override the fear and take that first step, that we can break free from its clutches and propel ourselves forward towards growth, success, and a life lived without regrets. Faith (belief and confidence) in yourself along with inspired action are the antidotes to fear. Like a muscle, it must be grown over time, especially if you come from a family heavily afflicted by fear or if you watch a 24-hour news channel daily! It was the application of Bob Proctor's information in *The Secret* that first made the intervention for Mark. Then, aligned with Equilibria's personal intervention, this has helped both authors on several occasions over the last two decades. At times, they have both physically hit the play button on their

E-Colours wristbands, and they could feel the weight of fear being lifted from their shoulders.

In sharing our journeys, we hope to inspire others to face their fears, embrace the unknown, and realise that there is nothing to fear but fear itself. You, too, have the power to overcome any challenge that comes your way. May both of their experiences serve as a testament to the indomitable human spirit and ignite the flame of possibility within those who dare to dream and take bold action towards success.

CHAPTER 6

~~~~~~

14 STEPS TO A WEALTHY MINDSET

STEP 13 - LEARNING FROM YOUR SUCCESS & FAILURES

"Success is not final; failure is not final: It is the courage to continue that counts."

– Winston Churchill,
former Prime Minister of the UK

Having a wealthy mindset involves learning from both successes and failures to continually improve and grow. Many people harbour fears of failure, while some fear success. Either approach can keep you stuck where you are.

Here are some key principles to keep in mind:

Embrace a Growth Mindset: Adopt a mindset that views failures as opportunities for learning and growth. Understand that setbacks are part of the journey and can provide valuable lessons to help refine your approach.

Reflect on Successes: When you achieve success, take time to analyse what worked well. Identify the strategies, actions, and decisions that contributed to your positive outcomes. This reflection will help you replicate and build upon your successes in the future.

Analyse Failures: Treat failures as learning events with valuable feedback rather than personal setbacks. For many, this comes with practice and learning to remove or manage emotional attachments to outcomes. Assess what went wrong, and identify the factors that contributed to the learning outcome. Be honest with yourself about your role in the failure, and use it as an opportunity to learn, grow, and improve. Don't let the fear of criticism, covered in the last chapter, stop you from trying something new. Remember, the master has failed more times than the beginner has even tried. Start acting towards your GOALS today.

Continual Learning: Cultivate a thirst for knowledge, and seek opportunities to learn and acquire new skills. Stay updated on trends, best practices, and strategies that can enhance your wealth-building efforts. Attend seminars and workshops, read books, take courses, and engage with coaches, mentors, and experts in relevant fields.

Take Calculated Risks: A wealthy mindset involves taking calculated risks and being comfortable with the possibility of failure. Assess the potential risks and rewards of an opportunity, and if the benefits outweigh the risks, act. However, ensure you have a plan in place and consider possible contingencies.

Build a Supportive Network: Surround yourself with like-minded individuals who share your wealthy mindset. Engage in discussions, exchange ideas, and seek guidance from those who have achieved success in areas you are pursuing. Learning from someone already living the way you aspire to live can help reduce time spent and avoid costly mistakes. A supportive network can provide valuable insights and motivation during both successes and failures.

Adjust and Iterate: Be flexible and willing to adjust your strategies based on the lessons learned from your successes and failures. Embrace experimentation and iteration as you refine your approach and adapt to changing circumstances. Recognise that the path to wealth is not always linear, and being adaptable is essential.

Looking back over the past two decades, here are some of the best decisions made by Mark and Paul:

1. Following the path of a wealthy mindset and achieving their GOALS.
2. Getting married and the birth of Paul's son.
3. Setting up their own businesses.
4. Tax optimisation.
5. Multiple sources of income with multiple revenue streams.
6. Diversifying revenue streams.
7. Diversifying investments—portfolio allocations.
8. Continuing to invest—always paying yourself first.
9. Prioritising expenses.
10. Staying out of debt.
11. Continually reviewing financial wealth and planning.

12. Continually developing learning and knowledge.

13. Not relying on the government, family, or friends for financial support.

14. Paul becoming a non-resident (wealth generation) and non-domiciled (wealth protection).

15. Investing in people.

Looking back over the past two decades, here are some of the failures that both Mark and Paul have learned from:

1. Dis-ease and bankruptcy (Mark's story, documented in *Life Remixed*).

2. Lending is often giving; it will not come back. Redefine "lending" as "giving."

3. Making several high-risk investments—15 in total—resulting in a USD 1 million loss. In hindsight, the risk was too high, and we trusted people too quickly.

4. Learning from some of the purchase of the condo/housing properties (17) over the last 20 years for various reasons. While not a negative return, a better ROI could have been achieved on some of these investments.

5. Buying a house to live in; financially, we would have been better off renting.

6. Buying expensive cars—limit these until you are financially independent, then you can afford it. Would I do it again? Yes, but only as part of my guilt-free spending when I am financially independent, and always recognise that you will be losing money.

7. Being too concerned about what other people think; it's none of our business and creates too much chaos and distraction. Forgive, forget, learn, and move on.

8. Being careful whom you trust—not everyone is looking out for your best interest.

Remember, developing a wealthy mindset is a lifelong journey. Embrace the process of learning from your experiences and continually evolving your approach. By doing so, you can enhance your chances of long-term success and wealth creation.

CHAPTER 6

⌒⌒⌒

14 STEPS TO A WEALTHY MINDSET

STEP 14 - DEVELOPING YOUR LEARNING & KNOWLEDGE

"I'm courageous enough to know I can accomplish great things. I'm humble enough to know when to ask for help."

– Katrina Mayer, motivational speaker

Continually developing your attitude towards learning and knowledge is crucial for maintaining a wealthy mindset. Your attitude is the result of aligning your thoughts, feelings, and actions. When these elements are misaligned, it can lead to mistakes, perceived failures, and even mental disorders or physical illnesses. This underscores the importance of studying personal development and committing to continuous learning and growth.

Adopting an attitude of gratitude, even for those situations or people you don't necessarily agree with, allows you the mental freedom to cultivate a learning mindset.

Here are some ways to cultivate this attitude:

Embrace Curiosity: Approach each day with a desire to learn something new. Cultivate a mindset that is open to exploring new ideas, concepts, and perspectives. Ask questions, seek answers, and be willing to challenge your existing beliefs. Remember, your thoughts become things, so resist the urge to judge too quickly. Instead, relax, explore, and stay curious and creative.

Pursue Lifelong Learning: Commit to lifelong learning and personal development. Engage in activities that expand your knowledge and skills, such as reading books, attending seminars, taking online courses, or participating in workshops. Continuously seek opportunities to enhance your understanding of wealth creation, finance, entrepreneurship, and personal growth. In addition, be visible and share your knowledge with others, whether through writing a book, public speaking, or developing your own learning programme.

Emphasise Self-Education: Take responsibility for your education, and proactively seek out the information you need to grow. Every day is a school day, so if you do find someone who 'thinks they know everything,' be careful! With the vast resources available today, such as books, articles, podcasts, videos, and online platforms, you have the tools to acquire knowledge in any area of interest. Understand your strengths and limitations, and over time, develop a habit of self-motivation, self-study, and staying proactive on your learning journey.

Embrace Challenges: View challenges as opportunities for growth and learning. Instead of shying away from difficult tasks, approach them with a positive mindset and a willingness to tackle the unknown. Embracing challenges helps you expand your knowledge and skills while building mental and emotional resilience and honing your problem-solving abilities.

Seek Diverse Perspectives: Surround yourself with diverse viewpoints, and engage in conversations with people from different backgrounds, cultures, industries, and those with varying personality styles. Exposure to varied perspectives broadens your understanding and challenges your assumptions and previous belief systems. It can also lead to innovative ideas and fresh insights that contribute to your wealth-building efforts.

Reflect and Review: Regularly reflect on what you've learned, and review your knowledge to reinforce it. Repetition is key to mastery. Once you learn something, you can't unlearn it, but you can forget it if you stop practising. As Gary Player famously said, "The more I practice, the luckier I get." This is the challenge for every individual. Summarise key points, create mind maps, or write journal entries to consolidate your understanding. Actively recall and apply what you've learned to reinforce your knowledge and make it practical. The majority of Life Remixed™ Coaching Clients stay involved well beyond the original "12 Months to Remix Your Life" coaching programme because the learning never ends.

Stay Current: Keep informed about the latest trends, developments, and changes in areas relevant to your financial wealth GOALS. Follow industry news, subscribe to newsletters, and join professional networks to stay updated. Being aware of the evolving landscape will enable you to adapt your strategies and make informed decisions.

Emphasise Practical Application: Apply the knowledge you gain to real-life situations. Seek opportunities to put your learning into practice, and experiment with different approaches. The combination of theory and practical application helps solidify your understanding and enables you to identify what works best in different contexts. In coaching sessions, Mark often says, as Bob Proctor advised, "Don't take my word for it; try these strategies yourself and see what happens." In every instance, something positive has occurred, as documented in the *Life Remixed* book and the many testimonials given to both authors for their work - www.markwilkinsonofficial.com/testimonials/ and www.hillmontassociates.com/testimonials

Remember, developing an open mind and an attitude for learning is an ongoing process. Don't be afraid to ask for help. Stay committed to continuous growth, seek out new opportunities to learn, and embrace the transformative power of knowledge on your wealth-building journey.

Asking for Help: This is a sign of strength and is crucial for developing a wealthy mindset. Here's why seeking assistance can be beneficial:

- **Gain New Perspectives**: Seeking help allows you to tap into the knowledge and experiences of others. Different individuals may have unique insights and perspectives that can broaden your understanding and provide fresh ideas. Their wisdom and guidance can help you navigate challenges and find new approaches to wealth creation.

- **Accelerate Learning**: Learning from someone who has already achieved success in areas you aspire to can accelerate your own learning curve. They can share valuable strategies, lessons learned, and practical tips that can save you time, effort, and potential mistakes. This can help you make progress faster and more efficiently.

- **Expand Your Network**: When you seek help, you connect with individuals who share your GOALS or have expertise in relevant areas. Building a network of coaches, mentors, advisors, or like-minded peers can provide ongoing support, accountability, and opportunities for collaboration. The connections you make can open doors to new possibilities and expand your wealth-building network. Mark has built the Life Remixed™ community in recent years, where the coaching client group helps each other to achieve their goals, alongside 1-2-1 coaching hours with Mark and global group calls and Book Clubs all held on Zoom.

- **Overcome Challenges**: No journey towards wealth is without obstacles. Seeking help when facing challenges allows you to access the knowledge and experiences of others who may have encountered similar situations. They can offer coaching, guidance, advice, and practical solutions to help you overcome obstacles and stay on track.

- **Boost Motivation and Accountability**: Asking for help provides an external source of motivation and accountability. When you involve others in your wealth mindset path, they can offer encouragement, support, and hold you accountable to your GOALS. This added support can help you stay motivated, focused, and committed to your journey.

- **Learn from the Mistakes of Others**: Seeking help allows you to learn from the mistakes of others. People who have experienced setbacks or failures can offer insights into what went wrong and how to avoid similar pitfalls. By learning from their experiences, you can make better-informed decisions and minimise potential risks.

Remember, asking for help is not a sign of weakness but a strong, proactive step towards growth and success. Be open to seeking coaching, guidance, mentorship, or advice from trusted sources who can contribute to your wealth mindset development. Whether it's through formal mentorship programmes, online communities, or personal connections, actively seek support and leverage the collective wisdom of others on your wealth-building journey.

Lastly, ensure you are gaining advice from the right sources. Everyone has an opinion, and many offer it without being asked. It's wise to listen to those who are succeeding in significant ways, decide if you appreciate their approach, and then choose which elements of their strategy and results you would like to implement in your own life.

CHAPTER 7

HOW IT ALL FITS TOGETHER THROUGH THE
14 STEPS TO A WEALTHY MINDSET

"As we express our gratitude, we must never forget that the highest appreciation is not to utter words, but to live by them."

– John F. Kennedy, former President of the United States of America

Developing a wealthy mindset and embracing life's abundance are key to the 14 Steps to a Wealthy Mindset. A wealthy mindset is not just about financial success; it involves cultivating beliefs, attitudes, and thought patterns that attract and create overall wealth. This mindset embraces a holistic view of abundance, covering not only monetary wealth but also personal fulfilment, well-being, and a strong sense of purpose. By integrating principles from personal development, mindset psychology, and financial wisdom, *Money Remixed* provides practical steps and insightful guidance to help individuals realise their full potential and achieve lasting wealth.

The 14 Steps cover these key principles:

Building a Holistic Wealth Framework: *Money Remixed* encourages redefining wealth to include financial prosperity, emotional well-being, fulfilling relationships, and a sense of purpose. It provides insights on how to align all areas of life to support and enhance financial abundance.

Cultivating Wealth Consciousness: Understand the power of visualisation, affirmations, and GOAL setting. Learn to programme your subconscious mind for wealth creation, creating a clear roadmap towards your life GOALS.

Ethical Compass: Navigate life's choices with integrity, using personal ethics as a guiding force for your daily actions. *Money Remixed* offers strategies for ethical decision-making that leads to a more meaningful and wealthy life.

Sustaining a Healthy Body and Mind: The book emphasises the connection between a healthy body and a sound mind, highlighting the importance of nurturing both as foundational elements for achieving success and fulfilment.

Shifting from Scarcity to Abundance: Learn to let go of scarcity-based thinking patterns, and embrace a mindset that sees opportunities and possibilities everywhere. Cultivating gratitude, optimism, and a sense of deservingness are key to attracting wealth and abundance.

Creating a Supporting Structure for Success: Understand the transformative power of surrounding yourself with individuals who possess a wealthy mindset. Harness the collective energy, knowledge, and inspiration of like-minded individuals to accelerate personal growth and expand possibilities.

Leveraging Personality Diversity: Recognise the unique personality traits, preferences, and communication styles of individuals. By understanding and adapting to different personality styles, you can enhance interpersonal skills, strengthen collaborations, and achieve remarkable results.

Effective Time Management: *Money Remixed* delves into the art of prioritising actions and explores the pitfalls of multitasking. It offers practical strategies to help you regain control of your time, enhance productivity, and achieve a greater sense of fulfilment.

Growing and Managing Financial Wealth: The book provides strategies and principles for long-term financial success and abundance. It serves as a guide to cultivating a wealth mindset, making informed financial decisions, and building a solid foundation for financial growth.

Managing Fear: *Money Remixed* offers strategies to manage and transcend the paralysing grip of fear, empowering you to move forward with confidence.

Embracing a Growth Mindset: This book emphasises the importance of continuous learning, adaptability, and resilience. It encourages embracing challenges, viewing both successes and setbacks as opportunities for growth, and committing to lifelong personal and financial development.

Asking for Help: *Money Remixed* highlights the importance of seeking help as a courageous act of self-awareness and humility. By embracing the power of asking, you can unlock resources, guidance, and opportunities that accelerate personal and professional growth.

By embracing the 14 Steps, you are invited on a transformative journey of self-discovery and empowerment. *Money Remixed* offers a robust framework through these 14 Steps, each designed to nurture a successful, wealthy mindset. The emphasis is on you adapting these steps to your unique circumstances and rigorously testing their effectiveness. By living and internalising these principles, you will embark on a rewarding path towards personal and financial prosperity, ultimately achieving profound satisfaction and fulfilment.

Having a wealthy mindset and access to money gives you choices, and the best choice of all is always to be able do what you like, when you like, and with whom you like.

CHAPTER 8

⌒

WHERE TO NEXT?

*"Don't dwell on what went wrong. Instead focus
on what to do next. Spend your energies on moving
forward towards finding the next answer."*

– Denis Waitley - motivational speaker

Rome stands as a testament to the resilience and vision of its architects and builders. Its grandeur did not materialise overnight but was the result of unwavering dedication and meticulous craftsmanship. It's amusing to ask Google how many days it took to build Rome. There are various answers, but it's clear it took far more than a day! Similarly, cultivating a wealthy mindset requires time, patience, effort, and a willingness to embark on a transformative journey. Within the pages of this book lie invaluable steps that will guide you towards unlocking the abundance you seek. Each step holds a key, waiting to be discovered and utilised. Embrace them with determination, and witness the foundations of your wealthy mindset gradually take shape. With *Money Remixed* as your compass, you have the power to construct a positive mindset and an empire of prosperity and fulfilment that benefits not only yourself but those around you—and possibly even the world.

Define Your Vision, Purpose, Value Creation & GOALS: At the heart of every successful journey lies a clear sense of purpose, a vision of added value creation, and well-defined GOALS. Embark on a transformative exploration of self-discovery, enabling you to create a roadmap to a wealthy mindset. By setting both short-term and long-term GOALS, and regularly revisiting and refining them, you establish a powerful framework that fuels your motivation, focus, and ultimate success.

Ethics: Ethics form the bedrock of personal conduct, professional behaviour, and societal contribution. Define and live by a set of principles that guide your actions and decisions. By doing so, you create a solid foundation for a life of purpose, fulfilment, and positive impact on others.

A Healthy Body & Mind: A healthy body and mind are invaluable assets that empower you to thrive in all areas of life. Choose to embark on a journey to understand the profound interplay between physical and mental well-being. By prioritising self-care, nurturing your body, and cultivating a resilient mind, you lay a solid foundation for success, enabling you to conquer challenges, embrace opportunities, and live a fulfilling life.

Desire & A Positive Mindset: Combining desire with a positive mindset creates a powerful synergy that propels you towards your GOALS. Your strong desire fuels your inspiration and motivation, while a positive mindset ensures you maintain resilience, overcome challenges, and stay focused on the wealthy mindset path. Reflect on your current beliefs and attitudes about wealth. Many people hold negative thoughts and feelings about money, such as "money is the root of all evil." In reality, money amplifies who you already are. If you're a good person, wealth can help you become even better (sadly, the reverse is also true). Identify any limiting beliefs or negative thoughts that may be holding you back. Reframe these beliefs, and cultivate a positive, abundant mindset. "There is more than enough" and "I can afford it" are two powerful mantras to help you change and grow. Commit to saying them out loud ten times each morning and evening until they become your truth. Embrace the belief that wealth is attainable and that you can create it.

Surround Yourself with People of a Wealthy Mindset: Surrounding yourself with people who have a wealthy mindset isn't about seeking perfection or avoiding all challenges. It's about creating a supportive and nurturing environment that fosters growth and resilience. Seek out a community of individuals who share your wealthy mindset GOALS, such as the 'Life Remixed™' Community, based in the UK with clients worldwide. Engage in discussions, attend networking events, and join online communities or mastermind groups focused on wealth creation. Surrounding yourself with like-minded individuals will provide support, accountability, and opportunities for collaboration and learning. Always be learning and growing.

Embrace Personality Diversity: In the vast tapestry of human existence, personality diversity weaves a vibrant and captivating pattern. In Ancient Greece, the philosopher Socrates famously declared that the unexamined life is not worth living. Asked to sum up what all philosophical statements could be reduced to, he replied: "Know thyself." Personality diversity gives us this gift and stands out as a profound force that can help shape our thoughts, feelings, actions, and interactions. Embrace the beauty and power of personality diversity. By delving into its depths and understanding its intricacies, you will uncover a transformative tool that acts as a positive multiplier towards a wealthy mindset.

Time Management: Effective time management involves making conscious choices about how you use the fixed time available to you. By setting GOALS, prioritising tasks, and organising activities, you can make the most of your time. This allows you to accomplish more, achieve your GOALS, and create a sense of balance in your life. Time management is really task management—ensuring you deliver on the most important tasks in the limited time you have will have the biggest impact on your wealth creation. It also reflects self-worth, knowing the value of your time.

Take Control of Your Finances: In the vast landscape of personal finance, taking control is the compass that guides you towards a future of abundance and security. The information shared in *Money Remixed* empowers you to embark on your journey of financial mastery, where you build wealth while safeguarding it with unwavering vigilance. It all begins with a deep dive into your current financial situation, peeling back the layers to reveal the true state of your affairs. Armed with this knowledge, you can then take deliberate steps to gain control over your finances, build your wealth, and protect it for the long term.

Managing Fear: Fear is a powerful force that can paralyse our actions, stifle our dreams, and hinder our progress. It infiltrates our minds, creating doubts and uncertainties that can hold us back from reaching our full potential. In the "Managing Fear" chapter, you embark on a transformative journey to understand the inner workings of fear and explore proven techniques to regain control of your life. By unravelling the mechanisms behind fear and equipping yourself with effective strategies, you can rise above your anxieties and embrace a life of courage, resilience, and limitless possibilities.

Learning from Your Successes & Failures: In the pursuit of success, our journeys are paved with both triumphs and setbacks. It is in these moments of achievement and failure that you have the greatest opportunity to learn, evolve, and thrive. Explore the profound wisdom that can be gleaned from both ends of the spectrum. By embracing a mindset of openness and adaptability, you unlock the transformative power of your experiences and embark on a path of continuous growth, innovation, and ultimate success.

Developing Your Learnings & Knowledge: In the development of a wealthy mindset, knowledge becomes the cornerstone of success. In "Developing Your Learnings & Knowledge," you embark on a transformative journey to expand your understanding of a wealthy mindset by committing to continuous learning through various sources. By doing so, you build a solid foundation of knowledge that empowers you to make informed decisions, embrace opportunities, and unlock your full potential. One of the keys to continued development is never being afraid to ask for help. Remember, fear will stop you from achieving, and help can come in many forms, including from your coach, your mastermind group, networking events, book clubs, podcasts, audiobooks, written books, and documentaries, to name but a few.

*   *   *

Remember, developing a wealthy mindset is a journey—it's a marathon, not a sprint. It takes time and consistent effort. Impatience is a form of fear, so be patient, stay focused on your GOALS, and celebrate the small victories along the way. With dedication and perseverance, you can create a wealthy mindset that aligns with your desires.

You must also learn to celebrate other people's successes and defend their right to be successful. If you ever find yourself in a position of jealousy or envy, you will remain there, consumed by negative emotions. We hope to have started you on that journey by sharing our experiences and advice in this book.

Remember the quote from the contents page: "Wealth is largely the result of habit" (John Jacob Astor, business magnate). You have the information in this book to follow a wealthy mindset, and financial wealth will follow as part of your journey. You just need to make the 14 Steps part of your habits.

For now, as we part ways in *Money Remixed*, we leave you with a reminder that choosing to seek help is a powerful and courageous act. It is a testament to your commitment to personal growth and development. This is what the authors do, and do not do, in order to gain financial wealth. It's what they consider to be "financial discipline":

We do:

1. Follow the 14 Steps to a Wealthy Mindset – COMMITTED as opposed to INTERESTED.

2. Prioritise our Needs, followed by Investing, followed by Wants.

We do not:

1. Purchase our houses, cars, or designer brands to keep up with others.

2. Go on holidays to flaunt wealth; we go where we can afford and want to go.

3. Eat in restaurants based on others' expectations; we eat where we want, enjoy, and can afford.

As a parting gift, we offer a further list of reading, listening, and viewing materials (in alphabetical order) that have served as our guiding lights on the journey of a wealthy mindset. This compilation will continue to evolve as we unearth new gems of wisdom. Embrace these resources with an open mind and an insatiable thirst for knowledge, for they hold the potential to inspire, educate, and transform your life. May they propel you forward, shaping your thoughts, expanding your perspectives, and fostering the limitless potential within you.

Remember, in your quest for growth, never underestimate the power of asking for help. *Money Remixed* is our way of offering that help, giving you a different perspective than you might hear most of the time.

List of Reading, Listening, and Viewing Materials (in alphabetical order)

Nine Things Successful People Do Differently, by Heidi Grant Halvorson
This inspiring and insightful book offers a roadmap for achieving success across various facets of life. Written by a personal development expert, it identifies nine key behaviours and habits common to highly successful individuals.

13 Secrets of World Class Achievers, by Vic Johnson
This empowering work unveils the strategies and mindsets employed by highly successful individuals across diverse fields. Through extensive research and interviews with accomplished figures, the author reveals 13 key principles that underpin the achievements of world-class performers. The book delves into traits such as goal setting, discipline, resilience, continuous learning, and time management. Each secret provides practical guidance and actionable steps for readers to apply, offering a comprehensive roadmap for both personal and professional success.

An Open Heart: Practicing Compassion in Everyday Life, by Dalai Lama, Nicholas Vreeland, and Khyongla Rato
Co-authored by His Holiness the Dalai Lama, Nicholas Vreeland, and Khyongla Rato, this profound book rooted in Tibetan Buddhism serves as a guide to cultivating compassion and kindness in daily life. Through insightful discussions and practical exercises, the authors explore how compassion can transform both individuals and society. They offer wisdom on developing an open heart, overcoming self-centredness, and fostering genuine care and concern for others.

As a Man Thinketh, by James Allen

First published in 1903, this classic work explores the profound influence of thoughts on character, circumstances, and overall quality of life. Allen presents the idea that our thoughts shape our reality and that we have the power to control and direct them. Through eloquent prose and reflections, Allen emphasises the importance of cultivating a positive and disciplined mind, asserting that our thoughts are the seeds from which actions and outcomes grow. By choosing thoughts consciously and nurturing a mindset of positivity, we can shape our destiny and attract abundance and success.

Atomic Habits, by James Clear

In this groundbreaking book, Clear reveals how minuscule changes can lead to life-altering outcomes. He uncovers simple life hacks, such as the forgotten art of Habit Stacking, the unexpected power of the Two Minute Rule, and the trick to entering the Goldilocks Zone. The book delves into cutting-edge psychology and neuroscience to explain why these techniques matter, sharing inspiring stories of Olympic gold medallists, leading CEOs, and distinguished scientists who have used the science of tiny habits to stay productive, motivated, and happy.

At the End of the Day: How One Man Learned to Live Like He Was Dying, by Lewis Senior, Laura M. Senior Garcia, and T.J. Bennett

For anyone struggling to balance life, family, and career while avoiding conflict, *At the End of the Day* is a must-read. The story centres on Lewis Senior, a workaholic who co-founded the international coaching company Equilibria. Believing he had taken his last breath on the floor of a French hotel room, Senior made a vow to change everything about his life. The book reveals the lessons he learned, including that unhappiness is a choice, suffering is optional, and circumstances are meaningless—it's how you respond that makes all the difference.

Baby Steps Millionaires, by Dave Ramsey

After decades of guiding millions through his plan, Ramsey proves that Baby Steps not only work for everyone but also work quickly. *Baby Steps Millionaires* doesn't reveal the secrets of the rich or complex concepts reserved for the elite. Instead, it offers straightforward, practical advice. The life you lead by following the Baby Steps is anything but boring, proving that you don't need a large inheritance or the winning lottery number to become a millionaire. This book is for anyone ready to get out of debt and build wealth—today.

Building Trust: In Business, Politics, Relationships, and Life, by Robert C. Solomon and Fernando Flores

In any significant relationship, whether in business, politics, or marriage, trust is the essential precondition for real success. *Building Trust* addresses what trust is, how it can be achieved and sustained, and most importantly, how it can be regained once broken. Solomon and Flores argue that trust is not a static quality but an emotional skill, built and sustained through promises, commitments, and integrity. The book offers invaluable insight into building authentic trust in an increasingly complex world.

Dirty Money, Netflix

Dirty Money is a compelling documentary series on Netflix that uncovers the layers of corporate greed, corruption, and financial fraud. Each episode takes viewers on a gripping journey into the dark underbelly of the global financial system, revealing how powerful individuals and institutions exploit loopholes and engage in illicit activities for personal gain.

E-Colours & Personal Intervention, by Equilibria Services Pte Ltd

This guide is an excellent resource for those interested in learning more about personality diversity. As social beings, we encounter various personality styles in our daily interactions. How we communicate with and influence others determines our success and satisfaction. The personality diversity tools presented in this guide allow you to be intentional about your interactions and plan positive outcomes, both individually and within a team, organisation, or community. The E-Colours process helps identify different personality styles, leading to a heightened awareness that we all have different communication styles and behavioural tendencies. Understanding and managing these tendencies through Personal Intervention can enhance individual, team, and organisational performance.

Feel the Fear and Do It Anyway, by Susan Jeffers

Are you afraid of making decisions, asking for a raise, leaving a relationship, or facing the future? In this enduring work of self-empowerment, Dr Susan Jeffers shares dynamic techniques that have helped countless people confront their fears and move forward. This updated edition addresses the post-pandemic world, offering strategies to raise self-esteem, become more assertive, connect with inner power, and create more meaning and enjoyment in life. Dr Jeffers shows how to become powerful in the face of fear, enabling you to live a creative, joyous, and loving life.

Focus, by Al Ries

What's the secret to a company's continued growth and prosperity? Marketing expert Al Ries provides the answer: focus. His common-sense approach to business management is founded on the premise that long-lasting success depends on focusing on core products and avoiding the temptation to diversify into unrelated enterprises. Using real-world examples, Ries shows that companies that resist diversification and focus instead on owning a category in consumers' minds tend to dominate their markets. He offers solid guidance on how to get focused and stay focused, providing a blueprint for increasing market share and ensuring future success.

From Strength to Strength, by Arthur C. Brooks

In the first half of life, ambitious strivers embrace a simple formula for success: focus relentlessly, work tirelessly, sacrifice personally, and climb the ladder without pause. This approach works—until it doesn't. In middle age, many find that success becomes elusive, rewards less satisfying, and relationships wither. They often double down on work to stave off decline, leading to anger, fear, and disappointment at a stage of life they expected to be filled with joy and fulfilment. *From Strength to Strength* offers a way out of this "strivers' curse." Happiness expert and best-selling author Arthur C. Brooks shares counterintuitive strategies drawn from science, philosophy, theology, and history to help release old habits, embrace new practices, and accept the gifts of the second half of life with grace, joy, and purpose.

Get Smart with Money, Netflix

Whether you're new to personal finance or looking to deepen your understanding, *Get Smart with Money* offers valuable insights and actionable advice to help you make informed decisions. This Netflix series encourages viewers to take control of their financial futures, adopt a mindset of abundance, and work towards long-term financial stability and prosperity.

Get the Edge, by Geoff Beattie

Geoff Beattie offers easy-to-follow advice on improving your relationships with yourself and others, sometimes in mere seconds. With impressive insights into what makes us tick, Geoff provides quick tips to help you shake off old, bad habits and quickly adopt new, positive ones. Whether you need to lift yourself out of a bad mood, spot a liar, get your partner to clean the house, or tell a joke well, this book gives you the edge.

Give and Take, by Adam Grant

The motivations behind today's most successful leaders and entrepreneurs can be traced to one decisive factor: some people give, some take, some match, and some fake. In a world filled with givers, takers, matchers, and fakers, it's the givers who succeed. *Give and Take* reveals the secrets behind the success of givers, such as Jack Welch, Richard Branson, and Jon Huntsman Sr. In a world where takers like Bernard Madoff have ruined lives, this book reassures readers that real power lies in becoming a giver. Grant not only explains why givers win but also shares their hidden strategies for achieving success.

Good to Great, by Jim Collins

After a five-year research project, Jim Collins concludes that good to great can happen and often does. In this book, Collins uncovers the underlying variables that enable organisations to leap from good to great while others remain merely good. Supported by rigorous evidence, his findings are surprising—sometimes even shocking—to the modern mind. *Good to Great* achieves a rare distinction: a management book full of vital ideas that reads as well as a fast-paced novel. It's widely regarded as one of the most important business books ever written.

How to Get Rich, Netflix

It's time to spring clean your spending habits. Finance expert Ramit Sethi meets with various individuals seeking financial intervention—a woman who spends half a million dollars a year on shopping, a couple involved in multilevel marketing and stock trading, a man with a checking account for his dog but no 401(k), and more. By helping them confront their relationships with money, Sethi enriches their lives.

How to Get Rich, by Felix Dennis

Felix Dennis believes that almost anyone of reasonable intelligence can become rich, given enough motivation and application. *How to Get Rich* is a distillation of his business wisdom, focusing on the step-by-step creation of wealth. Part manual, part memoir, this book ruthlessly dissects the business failures and financial triumphs of a "South London lad who became rich virtually by accident." It serves as an invaluable guide for those willing to stare down failure and transform their lives.

How to Win Friends and Influence People, by Dale Carnegie
This timeless self-help classic, first published in 1936, offers practical advice and techniques for building strong interpersonal relationships, winning people over, and effectively influencing others. Carnegie's principles are grounded in understanding human nature, empathy, and the power of positive interactions. The book provides strategies that can be applied daily, emphasising genuine interest in others, active listening, and offering constructive feedback and encouragement.

I Am Not Your Guru, Netflix
This documentary provides a behind-the-scenes look at Tony Robbins' popular event, "Date with Destiny," offering an intimate portrayal of Robbins as he guides individuals through deep introspection. The film showcases Robbins' ability to empower participants to confront their fears, break through limiting beliefs, and create positive change in their lives. Through intense, emotionally charged exercises, Robbins challenges participants to discover their true selves and unleash their untapped potential.

Influence: The Psychology of Persuasion, by Robert B. Cialdini
Cialdini explains the psychology behind why people say yes and how to apply these insights ethically in business and

everyday settings. Through memorable stories and relatable examples, Cialdini makes this crucial subject surprisingly easy to understand. His Universal Principles of Influence—Reciprocation, Commitment and Consistency, Social Proof, Liking, Authority, Scarcity, and the newest principle, Unity—are tools to become a more skilled persuader and defend against unethical influence attempts.

It's Not About the Money, by Bob Proctor

Renowned personal development coach Bob Proctor explores the relationship between money and personal fulfilment, challenging the belief that money alone is the key to happiness. Proctor suggests that our mindset and beliefs about money significantly impact our financial outcomes. He delves into the psychological and emotional aspects of money, helping readers overcome limiting beliefs and develop a healthy relationship with money. Proctor's book goes beyond financial advice, offering insights into personal development, fulfilment, and the power of the subconscious mind.

Life Remixed - A Modern Self-Development Book: Looking Beyond the Dance to Face the Music, by Mark Wilkinson

Endorsed by Bob Proctor and Marci Shimoff, contributors to *The Secret*, *Life Remixed* is a straightforward, modern-day self-help book. It's designed for those suffering from addiction, health, relationship, or financial challenges, or anyone feeling stuck in a rut and ready to re-evaluate their life. The book shows you how to remix your life and unlock the ability to make significant changes.

Moonwalking with Einstein, by Joshua Foer

Foer explores the fascinating world of memory and delves into the techniques used by memory champions to achieve extraordinary feats of recall. The book chronicles Foer's journey from being a journalist covering a memory competition to becoming a participant himself. He shares his experiences with renowned memory experts and introduces mnemonic techniques like the memory palace, which allow individuals to store and recall information with remarkable accuracy.

One Million Followers, by Brendan Kane

In a world where over 60 billion online messages are sent daily, *One Million Followers* teaches you how to make a significant impact in the digital world and stand out among the noise. Digital strategist Brendan Kane, who has built online platforms for A-listers like Taylor Swift and Rihanna, shares his secrets for gaining an authentic, dedicated, and diverse online following from scratch. Kane provides a 30-day plan to create personal, unique, and valuable content that will engage your core audience and build a multimedia brand across platforms like Facebook, Instagram, YouTube, Snapchat, and LinkedIn.

The Mind Explained, Netflix

This enlightening docuseries produced by Netflix takes viewers on a captivating journey into the complexities of the human mind. With a compelling blend of scientific research, expert interviews, and engaging visuals, the series seeks to unravel the mysteries of our thoughts, emotions, and behaviours.

Rich Dad Poor Dad, by Robert Kiyosaki

Kiyosaki shares personal experiences and lessons learned from his two influential father figures: his own dad, referred to as the "poor dad," and the father of his best friend, known as the "rich dad." The book challenges conventional beliefs about money and provides readers with valuable insights into financial literacy, wealth creation, and the mindset required to achieve financial independence. It encourages individuals to question societal norms and traditional education when it comes to financial matters. Through engaging storytelling, Kiyosaki introduces readers to key financial concepts such as assets, liabilities, cash flow, and passive income. He emphasises the importance of financial education, taking calculated risks, investing wisely, and learning from both successes and failures. The book ultimately outlines how individuals can escape the "rat race" by making informed financial decisions and striving to attain financial freedom.

Spark, by John J. Ratey

In *Spark*, John J. Ratey presents scientific evidence and compelling research that supports the notion that physical exercise not only benefits the body but also has profound effects on the brain. He delves into the impact of exercise on various aspects of cognitive function, mental health, and overall well-being. Ratey explores how exercise enhances learning, improves memory, boosts creativity, and increases attention span. He explains the physiological mechanisms behind these cognitive benefits, including the release of neurotransmitters, the growth of new neurons, and the improvement of brain plasticity. Moreover, *Spark* sheds light on how exercise positively influences mental health conditions such as depression, anxiety, and ADHD. It discusses the role of exercise as a natural antidepressant and mood regulator, highlighting the potential of physical activity as a powerful adjunct to traditional therapies.

Start with Why, by Simon Sinek

Why are some people and organisations more inventive, pioneering, and successful than others? And why are they able to repeat their success again and again? According to Simon Sinek, the reason is simple: it doesn't matter what you do in business. What matters is why you do it. In *Start with Why*, Sinek explains how leaders like Steve Jobs, the Wright brothers, and Martin Luther King shared a common trait—they all started with why. This book is for anyone who wants to inspire others or to be inspired themselves.

The 22 Immutable Laws of Marketing, by Al Ries & Jack Trout

As world-renowned marketing consultants and best-selling authors of *Positioning*, Al Ries and Jack Trout explore the fundamental rules that govern successful marketing. They argue that just as physics has laws, so too does marketing, and ignoring these laws can lead to failure. In *The 22 Immutable Laws of Marketing*, Ries and Trout offer a comprehensive guide to understanding and succeeding in the global marketplace. From the Law of Leadership to the Law of the Category and the Law of the Mind, these insights have stood the test of time and present a clear path to building and maintaining successful brands. The authors stress that violating these laws can result in marketing disasters.

The E-Myth Revisited, by Michael E. Gerber

In this revised edition of his best-selling book, Michael E. Gerber dispels the myths surrounding starting your own business and shows how commonplace assumptions can get in the way of running a successful enterprise. He walks readers through the stages in the life of a business, from entrepreneurial infancy through adolescent growing pains to the mature entrepreneurial perspective that is the guiding light of all businesses that succeed. Gerber shows how to apply the lessons of franchising to any business—whether it is a franchise or not. Finally, he draws the vital, often overlooked distinction between working on your business and working in your business. After reading *The E-Myth Revisited*, you will be equipped with the knowledge to grow your business in a predictable and productive way.

The Millionaire Mind, by Thomas J. Stanley & William D. Danko

Building on the success of *The Millionaire Next Door*, *The Millionaire Mind* delves into how America's wealthy really think and act, and how they became so successful. In this audio programme, you'll discover surprising answers to questions like: What success factors made them wealthy in one generation? What role did luck and school grades play? How do they find the courage to take financial risks? How did they find their ideal vocations? What are their spouses like, and how did they choose them? How do they run their households, buy and sell their homes, and what are their favourite leisure activities? To become a millionaire, you must think like one—*The Millionaire Mind* tells you how.

The Monk Who Sold His Ferrari, by Robin Sharma

The Monk Who Sold His Ferrari encourages readers to prioritise self-care, simplify their lives, and cultivate a more balanced and meaningful existence. It emphasises the importance of mindfulness, gratitude, and living in the present moment to find inner peace and fulfilment. The book offers practical exercises and actionable advice for implementing positive changes in one's life. It encourages readers to reflect on their values, reassess their priorities, and make conscious choices that align with their true purpose and aspirations. While *The Monk Who Sold His Ferrari* is a work of fiction, it draws upon real-life principles and teachings from various spiritual traditions. It aims to inspire readers to lead more authentic and purpose-driven lives, breaking free from the trappings of materialism and societal expectations.

The Outsiders: Eight Unconventional CEOs and Their Radically Rational Blueprint for Success, by William N. Thorndike

The Outsiders profiles eight CEOs who were considered "outsiders" in their industries, meaning they didn't conform to traditional management practices or follow conventional wisdom. Instead, they embraced unique perspectives and took bold, unconventional actions that led to significant success for their companies. The book examines the leadership styles and strategic decisions of these CEOs, including Warren Buffett of Berkshire Hathaway, John Malone of TCI, and Katharine Graham of The Washington Post Company. Thorndike highlights their rational and long-term approach to decision-making, capital allocation, and shareholder value creation. He analyses the specific strategies employed by these CEOs, such as focusing on cash flow, decentralised decision-making, prudent risk-taking, and capital discipline. Thorndike demonstrates how these unconventional approaches contributed to the exceptional performance and shareholder returns achieved by the companies under their leadership.

The Richest Man in Babylon, by George S. Clason

Originally published as a series of pamphlets in the 1920s, *The Richest Man in Babylon* presents timeless financial principles through a collection of parables set in ancient Babylon. The book revolves around stories and teachings that offer valuable lessons on wealth accumulation, financial management, and prosperity. It follows the lives of various characters, including Arkad, the titular "richest man in Babylon," who imparts his wisdom and insights on achieving financial success. Through these stories, Clason highlights key principles such as saving a portion of income, investing wisely, living within one's means, and cultivating sound financial habits. The book emphasises the importance of taking personal responsibility for one's financial well-being and making informed decisions about money. Despite being set in ancient times, the principles in *The Richest Man in Babylon* remain universally applicable and relevant in today's modern world.

The Rich Rules: Steps to Wealth & Happiness, by Kevin Green

Do you wish to become wealthier and happier? If the answer is yes, then this is the book for you. Whether you are thinking of starting or improving a business, Kevin Green's life experiences in *The Rich Rules* provide you with the essential strategies for achieving success. Kevin Green, once homeless, is now a multimillionaire businessman who cares passionately about giving back to the community. Kevin is an ambassador for Make-A-Wish UK, a charity that grants magical wishes to children and young people fighting life-threatening conditions.

The Secret, by Rhonda Byrne – Apple TV or Amazon Prime

The Secret reveals what the author describes as the most powerful law in the universe. This knowledge has been passed down through the ages, running like a golden thread through the teachings of prophets, seers, sages, and great men and women throughout history. Byrne explains the law that governs all lives and offers the knowledge of how to create a joyful life—intentionally and effortlessly. *The Secret* suggests that by understanding and applying this law, every human being can transform any weakness or suffering into strength, power, perfect peace, health, and abundance. This is the secret to everything—unlimited happiness, love, health, and prosperity. *The Secret* aims to reveal the secret to life.

The Science of Getting Rich, by Wallace D. Wattles

Initially published in 1910, *The Science of Getting Rich* is a classic work that explores the principles of wealth creation and the mindset required to achieve financial success. Wattles emphasises that becoming rich is not a matter of luck or circumstance but a result of following certain principles and adopting a specific mindset. He argues that there is a science to getting rich, and anyone can achieve financial abundance by understanding and applying these principles. The book emphasises the power of thoughts and beliefs in attracting wealth. Wattles suggests that by focusing on abundance and maintaining a positive mindset, individuals can tap into the creative power of the universe and manifest their desires. However, he also emphasises that thoughts and beliefs must be accompanied by purposeful action to create tangible results. Throughout the book, Wattles covers various aspects of wealth creation, including the importance of gratitude, the proper use of visualisation, the role of creativity, and the need for perseverance. He also addresses the concept of competition, asserting that wealth creation does not require taking away from others but rather involves creating value and contributing to society.

The Way of the Superior Man, by David Deida

The Way of the Superior Man is a guidebook that explores the concept of masculinity and offers insights and advice for men seeking to live authentically and fulfil their highest potential. In this book, Deida delves into various aspects of a man's life, including relationships, purpose, spirituality, and sexuality. He explores the challenges that men face in these areas and offers perspectives and practices to navigate them with wisdom and integrity. The book challenges traditional notions of masculinity and encourages men to embrace their deepest purpose and truth. Deida emphasises the importance of self-awareness, self-mastery, and a willingness to confront one's fears and limitations in order to grow and evolve as a man. Throughout the book, Deida discusses topics such as communication, intimacy, emotional intelligence, and the dynamics of masculine and feminine energies in relationships. He provides practical advice for cultivating healthy and fulfilling partnerships while also highlighting the importance of maintaining one's individuality and personal growth.

Think and Grow Rich, by Napoleon Hill

Think and Grow Rich is considered one of the most influential books on personal success and wealth creation. Drawing from interviews with successful individuals, Hill presents a philosophy and practical techniques for achieving financial abundance and personal fulfilment. The central premise of *Think and Grow Rich* is that one's thoughts and mindset have the power to shape their reality. Hill emphasises the importance of having a clear and burning desire for success, backed by a strong belief in one's abilities. He introduces the concept of the "mastermind," highlighting the value of surrounding oneself with like-minded individuals who can provide support, guidance, and collaboration. Throughout the book, Hill explores various principles and strategies for achieving wealth and success. He covers topics such as setting clear goals, developing persistence and resilience, cultivating a positive mental attitude, and harnessing the power of imagination and visualisation. Hill also emphasises the importance of taking decisive action and maintaining a continuous learning mindset. While the book is titled *Think and Grow Rich*, Hill's definition of wealth encompasses more than just financial riches. He argues that true success involves a harmonious balance between financial prosperity, personal relationships, spiritual growth, and overall well-being.

Transactionalism: An Historical and Interpretive Study, by Trevor J. Phillips, John Patterson & Kirkland Tibbels

Transactionalism: An Historical and Interpretive Study is the result of a search to find an answer to the seemingly simple question: "What is transactionalism?" Before this writing, transactionalism had no codified or single source of reference, yet the term has been described and explained fairly consistently across numerous fields of study. Transactionalism is a set of philosophical tools, or a method, employed to address the complexities of human social exchange or transactions. It is a method of inquiry or approach that has been studied and applied to various disciplines, including philosophy, education, psychology, political science, economics, and social anthropology.

Unleash the Power Within, by Tony Robbins

How do you really want to live? What are you most excited about? What are you grateful for? Do you often feel "stuck" in your life? Are you unable to make changes or break through past beliefs? In *Unleash the Power Within*, Tony Robbins teaches you how to transform your limiting beliefs and add new meaning and depth to your life. He helps you tap into your deepest resources to become all you truly desire and deserve. Robbins shows how to live life not by hope or chance but by design. This live audio seminar aims to equip you with the tools to make a remarkable improvement in your life and, by extension, in the world around you.

Willpower: Rediscovering the Greatest Human Strength, by Roy F. Baumeister, Denis O'Hare, and John Tierney

Pioneering research psychologist Roy F. Baumeister collaborates with *New York Times* science writer John Tierney to revolutionise our understanding of self-control, one of the most coveted human virtues. *Willpower* draws on cutting-edge research and the wisdom of real-life experts to offer lessons on how to focus your strength, resist temptation, and redirect your life. The book shows readers how to be realistic when setting goals, how to monitor progress, and how to maintain faith even when faltering. By blending practical wisdom with recent scientific research, *Willpower* makes it clear that whatever we seek—whether happiness, good health, or financial security—we won't reach our goals without first learning to harness self-control.

You Can Heal Your Life, by Louise L. Hay

Louise Hay's key message in this powerful work is that "If we are willing to do the mental work, almost anything can be healed." Hay explains how limiting beliefs and ideas are often the cause of illness and how changing your thinking can improve the quality of your life.

Your Brain at Work, by David Rock

In *Your Brain at Work*, David Rock takes readers inside the minds of Emily and Paul as they attempt to manage the vast quantities of information they are presented with, figure out how to prioritise it, organise it, and act on it. Rock, an expert on how the brain functions, especially in work settings, shows readers how to not only survive in today's overwhelming work environment but to succeed in it while still feeling energised and accomplished at the end of the day. *Your Brain at Work* explores issues such as why our brains feel so taxed and how to maximise our mental resources, why it's so hard to focus and how to better manage distractions, how to maximise the chances of finding insights that can solve seemingly insurmountable problems, how to keep your cool in any situation to make the best decisions possible, how to collaborate more effectively with others, why providing feedback is so difficult and how to make it easier, and how to be more effective at changing other people's behaviour.

You Were Born Rich, by Bob Proctor

Bob Proctor, prominent speaker, author, and personal development coach, explores the concept of abundance and wealth consciousness in *You Were Born Rich*. The book guides readers to realise their innate potential for success and prosperity. Proctor's central premise is that every individual is born with unlimited potential and the ability to create a life of abundance. The book explains that true wealth is not solely determined by external circumstances but is rather a result of one's mindset, beliefs, and actions. *You Were Born Rich* provides practical strategies and exercises to help readers shift their mindset from scarcity to abundance. It explores topics such as goal setting, visualisation, affirmations, and the power of focused intention. The book emphasises the importance of taking responsibility for one's life and choices, encouraging readers to adopt a proactive approach to personal and financial success. Drawing upon various metaphysical principles, including the Law of Attraction and the power of the subconscious mind, Proctor explains how these principles can be harnessed to manifest desired outcomes and attract wealth and opportunities into one's life. Additionally, the book discusses the significance of self-awareness and continuous personal growth. It encourages readers to identify and overcome limiting beliefs and self-imposed barriers that may be hindering their progress. By developing a greater understanding of themselves and their potential, readers can unleash their inner power and create a life of abundance.

PAUL GRANT

Paul Grant is a seasoned entrepreneur, having established many successful ventures in the past 20 years, building his net worth to place him within the top 0.15% of the UK's wealthiest individuals. A graduate with First Class Honours in Civil Engineering from Heriot-Watt University in Edinburgh, Paul began his career in the Oil & Gas industry, where he held key positions including Drilling Engineer, Operations Engineer, Rig Manager, Country Manager, Division Manager, Director of Compensation, Human Resources Manager, Vice President of Human Resources, and Director of Marketing. His work has taken him across the globe, from the UK and West Africa to Asia, the Middle East, North and South America.

After transitioning from corporate roles, Paul founded his own companies with various partners, earning a reputation for building wealth, transforming workplace cultures, and driving productivity. He is also a certified E-Colours coach and has contributed to numerous materials on communication, leadership, teamwork, and safety management. Passionate about helping young professionals achieve financial success, Paul dedicates his time to mentoring people on wealth-building strategies.

When he's not working, Paul enjoys spending time with his family in Thailand. *Money Remixed* is his debut book, with *Personalities Remixed* and *Business Remixed* on the horizon.

MARK WILKINSON

Mark Wilkinson is a multiple business owner, coach, speaker, and published author. Originally, music was Mark's life as an inter- national house music DJ and record producer. He was resident DJ at the famed Ministry of Sound in London, played music in 65 different countries, and achieved a UK Top 10 hit!

At 33 years of age, Mark collapsed with an incurable disease. It was the start of a hellish experience as his body froze up over the next 18 months resulting in him being unable to walk. He was in constant agony and lived on painkillers. His loss of health and financial setbacks even- tually led to bankruptcy, depression, loneliness, and suicidal thoughts.

On a detox in Scotland, Mark was given a DVD of *The Secret*. In it, he learned from Bob Proctor that disease is two words: dis-ease. This brand-new information completely opened Mark's mind to new ways of thinking, feeling, and being. He began to study philosophy and personal develop- ment to detoxify and cure his body, eventually completing four marathons.

After hitting rock bottom, Mark took positive action, over- came his health issues, and re-educated himself in a new career in construction Health and Safety. He worked at the London Olympic Stadium for the 2012 Games and then at London Heathrow Airport as HSE Manager overseeing their entire commercial construction portfolio. He next became Head of HSE at a division of a residential home developer having overall HSE responsibility on a 90-acre, £1 billion project.

During this time, Mark Wilkinson was introduced to the UK's largest landlord and self-made millionaire, Kevin Green, and completed his Kevin Green Wealth (KGW) property wealth coaching programme. As a result, Mark was asked to join the KGW coaching team to share his knowledge of business, property investing, and wealth management.

In 2018, Mark set up his own Health and Safety consultancy, which meant he could also focus on his various property businesses and develop as a coach and speaker.

Mark Wilkinson's debut book *Life Remixed* launched in February 2021. The book tells the story of his roller coaster life as a DJ, how he lost everything, and how he remixed his life.

Mark is now a Fellow of the Institute of Leadership & Management (FInstLM) and a Chartered Member of the Institute of Safety and Health (CMIOSH). He holds an NVQ7 Master's in Strategic Management and Leadership (MPhil) and plans to study next for a PhD in Directional Leadership. He is also an E-Colours practitioner and coach.

For more information about Mark, please visit: www.markwilkinsonofficial.com www.liferemixed.co.uk

UPCOMING AND AVAILABLE 'REMIXED' BOOKS

Coming soon
Personalities Remixed – summer 2025
Business Remixed – winter 2025

Available now
Life Remixed
learn more:
www.markwilkinsonofficial.com/life-remixed/

Contact Mark & Paul to arrange a
Wealth Coaching consultation:
www.markwilkinsonofficial.com
Learn more about the **E-Colours**:
www.markwilkinsonofficial.com/e-colours/

Link to E-Colours PDI questionnaire
–there are 3 levels of the report –
Free, Basic or Premium
upgrade to Premium using
MONEYREMIXEDPREMIUM code for 20% off
www.equilibria.com/PDI-home/

Equilibria shop website for E-Colours
Practitioner Courses, Online E-Colours & Personal
Intervention Books, E-Colours Alignment Reports and
many more offerings:
www.shop.equilibria.com/shop?ref=nwvlztl

Equilibria website to learn more about
the history of E-Colours and
the coaching services provided:
www.equilibria.com

Mark Wilkinson Official LinkedIn
to learn more about the services offered:
www.linkedin.com/in/markwilkinsonofficial/

www.ingramcontent.com/pod-product-compliance
Lightning Source LLC
Chambersburg PA
CBHW070710190326
41458CB00004B/929